INDIAN SCOUT WESTERN PAINTER

Captain Charles L. von Berg

From the opening "rifle shot" until "bis dann" Paul K. Heerwagen brings Captain Charles L. von Berg back to life in his biography "Indian Scout—Western Painter". Having known the "Old Warrior" intimately in his late years and having visited and talked with him many times, Heerwagen's close association adds an authenticity to the book that could not otherwise have been achieved.

To most people, Charles L. von Berg is not known—at least not as well as his contemporaries Buffalo Bill Cody, Wild Bill Hickock, General Custer, Rain-in-the-face, Chiefs Sitting Bull and Yellow Horse. But in the winning of the West, his contributions were just as important as theirs, if not more so.

Linguist, explorer, hunter, fur-trader, soldier, guide, naturalist, scout, musician, taxidermist, hand-to-hand fighter—in all these he excelled. However, as a store-keeper and a farmer he was a dismal flop. As a family man he was not a paragon either, being considered more or less a "visitor" to his first wife, three sons and a daughter.

Truth often transcends fiction. No story of the "wild, wild west" or of "cowboys and Indians" that William Buntline ever wrote can compare with von Berg's story of the duel "to the death" he fought (and won) against Chief Yellow Dog of the Sioux. Von Berg was challenged as chief of the U. S. Army Scouts under General George Crook by Chief Yellow Dog of the Sioux under Chief Crazy Horse. They fought on neutral ground, von Berg with his gun "Old Betsy" and a knife, Crazy Horse with a tomahawk and a knife. The best man, von Berg, won—for the honor of the United States Army.

Indian Scout—

Western Painter

Hundreds of other stories—terse and carefully documented—are related by Paul Heerwagen in his biography of von Berg. Photographs of the "Old Warrior" and his friends are also included.

Born in Germany of a noble family —von Berg was almost forced by the revolution of 1848 to immigrate to the United States. From his readings he was entranced with the West. From Karlsruhe, Germany, where he was born, to "Ioway" where he and his family lived for many years, to Fayetteville, Arkansas, where he died, his wanderings and work led him a little bit of everywhere, particularly throughout the Indian territories of the West.

Simple, straightforward, factual, well-told, highly entertaining and interesting—and knowing the story to be the true story of an unusual man —one of those who in his own way helped immensely to build and secure his adopted country—is the best accolade that can be given to Paul K. Heerwagen's biography of Captain Charles L. von Berg, "Indian Scout— Western Painter".

Indian Scout— Western Painter

CAPTAIN CHARLES L. VON BERG

by

PAUL K. HEERWAGEN

PIONEER PRESS
LITTLE ROCK, ARKANSAS

Book Design By
C. ARMITAGE HARPER

Printed in U.S.A.

TO THE MANY
who supplied the threads of information
which enabled me to weave this biography

CONTENTS

ILLUSTRATIONS

Indian Scout—
Western Painter

CAPTAIN CHARLES L. VON BERG

I

Indian Scout
With Eight Names

A rifle shot exploded the dead stillness. The graceful little antelope nibbling at the buffalo grass sprang into the air from a four-footed stance.

A second rifle shot resounded at that instant. However the second report had a different sound for it was from another rifle.

The little antelope hit the ground, dead.

The Indian boy's expression was not the proverbial stoic look of an Indian but, like any boy, showed death fear as he looked into twinkly blue eyes, capped by a mop top of long brown hair which came down on broad shoulders. Those blue eyes portrayed part of his smile as he spoke to the boy in the Sioux language, "Hold your breath when you shoot, lad, so that you do not spoil your aim."

The Indian boy's fear somewhat subsided as he came out with what was uppermost in his mind, "You could have killed me."

Reassuringly, the Indian scout—for that was who he was—Captain Charles von Berg, better known to the Indians as "Eagletail"— said, "I don't shoot Indian boys and squaws. But let's take care of your antelope. First thing we have to do is gut him."

Side by side the Indian scout and the Indian lad walked down the slope to where the antelope lay. "Eagletail" stood by, meaning for the Indian boy to clean the kill. He did right well as the eyes of the scout showed approval of the technique the lad employed. When he had finished, the scout put his hand on the boy's shoulder, "I couldn't have done it better or quicker, lad."

This pleased the Indian boy as he relaxed for the first time with a grin of appreciation.

"Now go get your pony, and remember when you get to camp what you don't tell 'em they can't know."

The Indian boy smiled as he understood what the hunter meant and darted off to the timber where he had tethered his pony.

On his way he looked back and waved a most friendly wave which was just as exuberantly returned by the scout. When the Indian lad reached the spot of their stand he again looked back but to his astonishment the hunter was nowhere to be seen. But there lay the antelope.[1]

Many years later halfway up on East Mountain, which

---

(1) As related by the "Old Scout" to the author, "It's a secret I will take to my grave, the Indian Chief this lad became. And if I could have known, I still would have done as I did."

got its name from being east of the town of Fayetteville, Arkansas, this same Indian scout, white-haired now but his blue eyes still sparkling, was instructing a Boy Scout troop at their headquarters—a log cabin tucked into the bench of the mountain. The group was outside and the "Old Scout"[2] was endeavoring to get over to his Boy Scouts the art of walking, or rather padding, so as not to be heard.

"Bob,"[3] he addressed—in his slight German brogue—one of his scouts, "do you want to tell every living thing that you are out hunting for them? Now watch that you don't step on a twig that will snap or a rock that might roll. When you get home study how your cat walks.

"Charlie,"[4] calling out to another one of his Boy Scouts, "you are bigger than the other boys but you can still walk like a panther if you practice. Watch that you don't brush against limbs, unduly rustling the leaves or possibly cracking a branch."

Then the Scout Master proceeded to lecture the troop.

"When you are hunting, you slip up on your game. Come in on the leeward side. You can't go crashing through the woods and brush. You must weave your way through so that you don't sound any alarm.

"Of course, you boys are not going to be stalking Indians —we've taken care of that—but there will be other wars. I can see 'em coming. Germany is going to grow too big for her 'hosen'. Yah! What I've seen on the West Coast of the Orientals we will have to tangle with them, too. So it might be the saving, not of your scalp but of your neck, that you know how to pad. I learned from the Indians—the hard way.

"It's no laughing matter, Scouts," as he noticed the boys tittering.

---

(2)   Scoutmaster's certificate No. 5140 (The Minneapolis Sunday Tribune, January 7, 1912).

(3)   Dr. Robert R. Logan—Emeritus—University of Arkansas, Fayetteville, Arkansas.

(4)   Charles Boozer—Retired—Engineer with Westinghouse, Wilsonville, Oregon.

One of the Boy Scouts spoke up, "You said a German word."

With that the "Old Scout" laughed with them and then rattled off German fluently.

"That's all for today, boys. Next time I will show you how to crawl on your bellies like a snake through the brush."

The "Old Scout" was a man of many aliases. Not that he changed them purposely, the names just seemed to evolve.

His German name (he was born in Germany) was Carlos Ludwig von Berg.

He was in his late teens when he immigrated to the United States. Years later he answered the call for the War of the Rebellion. He enlisted under the name of C. Louis von Berg, which was anglicizing Ludwig.

After the war he took the name of Charles L. von Berg which he used in advertising his Guide and Hunter Service to the Rockies. Here, he was anglicizing Carlos.

As an Indian scout he acquired the rank of Captain in this way: The army had no provision for paying scouts more than a private's pay, so they were hired through the Quartermaster Corps in order to receive the remuneration to which they are entitled. Colonel Cody—Buffalo Bill—and Major North, both outstanding Indian scouts, acquired their ranks the same way.

The ones who knew him intimately changed Charles to Charlie and dropped the von, so he was Charlie Berg to them.

The Indians gave him the name of "Eagletail", for to the Indians the eagle was an indestructible bird. They couldn't kill an eagle with their bow and arrow. Certainly, to them von Berg was indestructible, because many a time had they tried to kill him.

His last sobriquet was "Old Scout" endearingly bestowed on him by his friends in Fayetteville, Arkansas where he retired.

Furthermore, he had an indirect alias. Indian scouts were secretive not only in the field, but their information was RESTRICTED to the Commanding Officer. Captain von Berg's resemblance to Buffalo Bill was so striking that many, many times he was mistaken for that grand showman of the mountains and the plains.

"KLEINER BUB" CARLOS LUDWIG

II

Kleiner Bub

The usual quietude and the restfulness throughout the Schwarzwald (Black Forest) in the Grand Duchy of Baden this night—Oct. 18, 1835[1]—were ajar.

It was a full moon—Hunter's Moon—which disturbed every living thing.

The lullaby from the sweep of the fir and pine branches was submerged by the pulse of restlessness.

The birds were upset and let it be known by their

(1) Date of birth—Carlos Ludwig von Berg. General Service Administration, National Archives and Records Service (certificate of Death), Family Register in Germany.

plaintive calls. The sheep bleated, cattle lowed, the horses stomped.

Lights shown here and there which ordinarily were not burning, indicating the insomnia of those wanting to sleep.

The old castle where lived the von Bergs[2]—chief foresters of the crown for generations[3]—was twinkling with lights from many windows. In the courtyard their livery coach swayed rather jerkily because the team of four didn't like being taken from their stalls and kept in readiness.

Down below the castle on a lane an entire family was standing on their stoop looking toward the castle. Presently a sharp-eyed German lad sang out, "There it is! It's a boy!"

All eyes riveted on a window in the turret in which flickered one candle. Which meant that the von Bergs had a new forester to perpetuate their lineage as Keepers of the Black Forest.

It was a German custom, these cycles of life portrayed by candles. For a boy child, the candle was set in the window. For a girl, a candle was set below the window ledge with only the light in evidence. Candles for the wedding night were mute evidence in the bridal chamber. Candles at the bier were appropriate to Freundliches Licht zu Spenden (Lead, kindly Light).

The Black Forest was the finest timber region of fir and pine in Germany. From it came the livelihood of many families either working in the woods or home manufacturing of many wood products from the timber of this forest region. Such home manufacturers were fine craftsmen, noted for their dexterity in wood carving. Their cuckoo clocks were quite symbolic of the Black Forest, as though in them were these birds brought from the woods which jubilantly cu-

---

(2) Sunday Magazine—St. Louis Post-Dispatch, Oct. 7, 1917.
Castle on the Rhine close by Karlsruhe, The von Bergs also had a home at Huffenhardt, north and east of Karlsruhe Bad. Generallandesarchiv, 75, Karlsruhe, 22 Juli 1965.

(3) Bad. Generallandesarchiv, 75, Karlsruhe, 22 Juli 1965. Courtesy of Consulate General of Germany in New Orleans.

ckooed the hours. The resonance they built into their music boxes of satin-finished wood was remarkable. Too, these artisans made ingenious wooden toys.

Then, the importance of timber improvement, protection from fires, supervision of cutting and reforestation were practiced so that their beloved Black Forest would not be depleted and become a worthless cutover area. The responsibility of the Black Forest was the von Bergs under the mandate of the Grand Duke.

Sometime later after the candle appeared in the window, could be heard the rhythmical clatter of the horses' hoofs and the gritty sound from the wheels of the von Berg's coach. In the moonlight, its coat of arms—three mountain peaks rising out of the foot of the shield and on the middle peak poised a chamois[4]—stood out as if embossed. The coach was traveling to Karlsruhe; and the lone passenger could easily be recognized as the doctor.

At the castle the midwife, who assisted, was having her coffee break. She remarked to the other servants in her company, "He's going to be a Wanderlust."

"Sh," softly spoke up one of the maids, "I wouldn't say that."

The older woman reiterated stoically, "Just wait and see. Anyone born under the 'Hunter's Moon' will be a Wanderlust. He'll never be the Keeper of the Black Forest."

Carlos Ludwig von Berg—so he was christened in Karlsruhe—inherited advantages of heredity and environment.

He was of the nobility.[5]

Reared in a healthy climate, for the Black Forest was so noted all over Europe, due to its elevation, for 80 percent

(4) Bad. Generallandesarchiv, 75, Karlsrhue, 22 Juli 1965, according to Ernst Heinrich Knesche, New General Book of Nobility, I, 1859, page 333.
Courtesy of Consulate General of Germany in New Orleans
(5) Same as above.

of the Grand Duchy of Baden is mountainous. In fact these foothills are of the Alps to the south in Switzerland. In addition, a healthy zest is added by the fir and pine forests. This is substantiated in that there were a number of famous watering places like the spa in Hot Springs, Arkansas. Baden—Baden was the most celebrated spa in Germany. It had hot springs for baths, parks, promenades and a brilliant social life in the casino. Somewhat parallel, the Romans came to these hot springs for their elixir; just as our Indians—all tribes laid down their bows and arrows—enjoyed the revitalization of the hot springs in Arkansas before the white men came.

Carlos remembered the "plush" of their sojourn to these watering places when he became old enough to accompany his father and mother. He recalled how proud he was of his handsome, military bearing father and the elegance of his mother as he "tagged along" on their promenades.[6]

The first thing that he remembered vividly of his early boyhood days was their Weihnachten (Christmas). How his father worked behind closed doors for weeks decorating for Christmas.[7] Whereupon, on Christmas Eve, the double doors were slid back and Carlos was invited to go in—to the accompaniment of Heilige Nacht (Holy Night) coming from a music box. Their beautiful little fir tree was aglitter with real candles and many shiny, delicate ornaments. At the base of the tree was the Nativity Scene. The host of

---

(6)   The author's father, Paul Martin Heerwagen, born 1866 in Germany, spoke, of course, his native tongue fluently. In 1911 we moved to Fayetteville, Ark. where my father met Captain von Berg. Mein vater, too, had that trait of "talk talk". I remember at our dining table his telling of meeting Captain von Berg. It made quite an impression on me when he said that Captain von Berg spoke "High Deutsch" for many times I had heard my father slurringly referring to others coming from Germany as speaking "Low Deutsch". He related that Captain von Berg told about being at Baden-Baden; and added that he, too, as a boy with his two older brothers and his mother and father would sojourn there.

(7)   The author's father told of Captain von Berg telling how his father spent weeks behind closed doors preparing for Christmas and then mein vater elaborated as to how his father also did this.

fluttering angels hovered over the manger. Each one was suspended by a fine thread which in the colored lights was invisible. The gossamer wings of these angels were of very thin membrane, which the heat from the candles on the tree caused their wings to expand and contract, thereby giving that lifelike flutter.[8]

His mother delighted in relating that when her boy was just a kleiner Bub (little shaver) desperately trying to catch rain drops and finally stalking into the castle soaking wet, dejected and exasperated, "Mother!" he called out, "the rain drops won't play fair. When I try to catch them, they spray me with water."

His father took Carlos with him on many enjoyable trips through the Black Forest, and it was there that he acquired his love for the woods and their wonderments. There he learned his forestry lessons, the habitats of wild life and botany species. How well these stayed with him was shown years later when he made a herbarium collection of wild flowers found in the Rockies.

His mother instilled into him the desire of wanting to read. Carlos would be transported in fantasy by her bedtime stories. One which he pleasantly recalled was about two lovers. The girl's father, a count, did not approve. So he took his daughter to the Pfalz Tower, which was in the middle of the Rhine.[9] (The Rhine was a reality to Carlos as it was the west boundary of the Duchy.) There she was kept prisoner from her lover. Not to be thwarted, her lover disguised himself as a pilgrim and gained access to the tower and his love. Later he took leave, rowing back to the bank;

---

(8) About Christmas Eve, which Captain von Berg described to him, mein vater really painted with words their Christmas was also, on Christmas Eve, which was a German custom, and that their decorations were far more elaborate. He described their Nativity Scene under the tree which revolved, a section showing the shepherds in the field, another the Wise Men following the Star and then the creche scene. Then he recounted as to their toys which were many and most ingenious. (His father represented a toy manufacturer and his samples—deleting the toys for girls—were given him for his boys.)

(9) Glimpses of the World—John L. Stoddard—1892.

however, instead of the pilgrim it was his lady-love disguised in his pilgrim cloak. That night he swam from the Pfalz and joined his fair lady hiding-in-waiting for him, and they lived happily ever after. The "Old Scout" in telling this story would add, "I've seen this Pfalz Tower. It's right there today in the middle of the Rhine."

Carlos's appreciation of music started with "Lullaby" from Erminie—Jakobowski[10] which his mother sang to him. Even when he outgrew the lullaby age he couldn't go to sleep until his mother—in her sweet soprano voice—had sung this lullaby.

Art, his mother started at an early age. She enraptured her boy with her description of "Holy Night"—Correggio— which she had seen in the Dresden Gallery.[11] Repeatedly, Carlos asked his mother to tell him about this famous painting. Her soulful description made this tender painting almost a reality. His mother's recountal started off with the Light that seemingly emanated from the Christ Child, brilliantly lighting the face of His adoring Mother who so tenderly had her arms protectively about her Divine Child. The Light washing the faces of the shepherd and shepherdesses was so strong that one of the shepherdesses shielded her eyes with one hand. The faithful shepherd dog, his ears back in wonderment, nuzzled up as closely as he could get to the crèche. The Heavenly Host of angels was spotlighted above by the Light as they gave their adorations. Joseph behind Mary was rather in the dim light as he restained the donkey. Both seemingly had the understanding that the safety of the Christ Child would be entrusted to them. Behind Joseph were the disquieted cattle being kept back by husbandmen.

At each conclusion, Carlos would ingeminate, "Mother! Some day, I'm going to paint."

He vividly remembered his tenth birthday present which was a trip with his mother and father to Oberammergau to see the Passions Spiele (Passion Play).[12] Years

---

(10) From the opera, "Erminie."
(11) Glimpses of the World—John L. Stoddard—1892.

later in relating this drama, Captain von Berg said, "It's like our Rockies, you not only see their grandeur but feel it."

Carlos Ludwig, like Achilles, must have been dipped several times in the River Styx to immunize him for life ahead.

He acquired endurance from walking many miles on his hikes through the Black Forest, even when the trees wore plumes of snow.

His equestrian lessons started early and like swimming stayed with him. For years later, whether he was getting the most from his famous horse, "Pawnee Bill" or riding a mule in the "Great American Desert"[13]—the plains—his life depended on outriding the Indians.

Mountain climbing in the Alps gave him the surefootedness and stamina that he had to have as guide to lead the way through the dangerous passes in the Rocky Mountains; as did the faithful Indian squaw guide, Sacajawea[14] in pointing the way to the passage to the Pacific; and as the famous scout and guide, Kit Carson[15] guided Lieutenant John C. Fremont on several expeditions in his explorations of "The unknown great West". The cycle was Lewis-Clark, 1803; Kit Carson, 1842; (both of these history making expeditions started from St. Louis) and Scout von Berg in the seventies.

Carlos had the advantage of attending schools in Karlsruhe. Here was located an outstanding polytechnic school which was Germany's finest preparatory school. The curriculum was amazing, considering that the time was over a hundred years ago. Besides languages—and English was one of them—courses were offered in mathematics, drawing, modeling, chemistry, mineralogy, geology and mechanics.

It is a conjecture but it appears that this background of

---

(12)   Given every ten years at Oberammergau, Bavaria.
(13)   Life on the Plains or Personal Experiences with Indians, General G. A. Custer, U. S. A.
(Sheldon & Company—1876)
(14)   Lewis-Clark Expedition.
(15)   Famous Frontiersmen, E. G. Cattermole. A. B., Courtesy University of Oklahoma Library.

seeking knowledge at Karlsruhe could be responsible for what is happening today. For the *Gesellschaft für Kernforschung,* a German corporation of Karlsruhe is cooperating with 17 investor-owned utility companies located in the South and Southwest, together with General Electric and the Atomic Energy Commission, in building and operating a fast oxide nuclear reactor.[16] Interestingly enough, it is located just 20 miles to the southwest of Captain von Berg's former home—Fayetteville, Arkansas.

The "Old Scout's" eyes shown with amusement as he related about the craniometrists who by examining with their hands the student's head, could determine his best aptitude. If their findings showed that the student's genius was that of a butcher, he was educated in that field.

"I imagine our universities would probably smirk at their method," he would conclude with that von Berg twinkle.

Then when someone would ask him what the craniometrists determined as to his head, he would just chuckle and chuckle and that was it.

Military training was an early must too, for Carlos. His military bearing stayed with him even though he had a slight limp. This came from a souvenir he carried in his leg—the tip of an arrowhead from a Blackfoot Indian.[17]

Carlos in his boy-formative period did not have Horatio Alger, Tom Swift, Rover Boys and Hardy Boys books. He yearned for adventure stories about the United States. He read everything about this new growing country he could "put his hands on". The Indians were his TV Westerns as he loved their nomad, outdoor way of living. His longing of wanting to go to America became an obsession.

Following his schooling at Karlsruhe, Carlos entered the

(16) Arkansas Democrat, Little Rock, Ark., Sunday Magazine Section, May 31, 1964.
(17) Arkansas Gazette, Little Rock, Ark., Sunday Edition, Nov. 1, 1964.

University of Heidelberg—a Protestant University—on the Neckar River just short of the Rhine.

He was not long at the University of Heidelberg, though he did come away knowing their stein song, "Ich hab mein Herz in Heidelberg verloren" (I've lost my heart at Heidelberg).

Because of the revolution which started in 1848—the liberals wanted to set up a German Union somewhat like the United States—Carlos was called home. The situation in the Duchy was getting out of the hands of the nobility. The French Revolution was still fresh in the minds of the Adel (nobility). The Grand Duke and his Gefolge (cortege) had to flee to Switzerland and this included the von Bergs. Some in coaches, some on horseback, some even afoot, through the grandeur of the Black Forest, the beauty of which went unnoticed, all were obsessed with the one thought of escape.

Carlos's mother was critically ill at the time. His father improvised a bed in their coach. With the senior von Berg attending her, Carlos drove the team of four. What to do when they came to the Upper Rhine which separated Germany from Switzerland was uppermost in Carlos's mind? They could leave the coach at the river bank and swim across on horseback easily enough, but Frau von Berg would not be able to sit on a horse. When they reached their last barrier, the Upper Rhine, it was not wide but it was still a river to cross. Carlos had the idea that if they would take the wheels off, the body of the coach would float for the doors fitted perfectly as they were dustproof. With the help of some of the refugees, the wheels were removed and they pushed the coach into the water. With Carlos riding one of the lead horses, the two spans supplied the horsepower for the crossing. Like a gondola the coach floated and presently emerged on the other side at Basel, Switzerland.

The trip probably was too much for Carlos's mother. Despite tender care of both husband and son, and the best doctors in Switzerland, Frau von Berg died.

During the ensuing year most of the nobility returned to Germany.

Carlos yearned to join the many German families leaving for America. These families were afraid of reprisal by the German nobility for their part in the rebellion.

Back to Heidelberg Carlos went. Its famous library gave him access to more information about America. After a couple of years there, he finally persuaded his father to let him go to America in company with a group who were friends and neighbors in the Duchy.[18]

So again through his beloved Black Forest he sojourned to Switzerland. Then they proceeded to Italy and from there took a boat for New York.

Enroute they put in at Lisbon, Brest and Cork to take on more immigrants.

The Germen's anticipation of a new start in a land of opportunities somewhat subdued their nostalgia of leaving their Vaterland. Carlos was the most enthusiastic of the immigrants. Due to his knowledge of America and having a propensity for "tall talk", his narrations and fantasies of the new world were hypnotic.

The accomodations aboard their good ship were sparse; and the ocean was rough at times, but all this was taken as a means to their reward to come.

An elderly German remarked with a chortle, addressing Carlos, "What I wouldn't give to be your age! It's a young country. You will grow up with it. Just remember, lad, laugh when it hurts." Captain von Berg laughed when he

---

(18) Author's note: I was 17 years old when I met Captain von Berg. I made many a trip to his lodge; never tiring of hearing him tell of his harrowing experiences. On one of these trips, it being uppermost in my mind why my father's family left Germany—because the oldest boy in one more year would have to go into the army, and as their father had died, his mother brought her three boys to America—I asked Captain von Berg why he had left the old country and that's when he related this at length.

recalled this incident, "I never forgot the old man's advice. Many a time when it looked like the Indians would take 'Eagletail's' scalp, I just laughed at 'em. Mind you, I was pumping lead into 'em at the same time."[19]

The day that land was sighted was a joyous one and songs from all quarters were heard. Each nationality tried to drown out the others with their national songs.

As the immigrants came close to where they could see their new home, it wasn't the Statue of Liberty which awed them for it was not there yet, but they all became reverently silent.

When the immigrants disembarked in October, 1854[20] they knelt in groups of their particular faiths and gave thanks for a safe voyage.

They moved away from the wharf in flocks, each nationality to themselves, not realizing that they would be absorbed in the great amalgamation which makes up the United States.

---

(19) The Old Scout told this to the writer and added, "I am passing this on to you, lad. It's as good today as it was when I was about your age."

(20) "It was on my birthday," chortled Captain von Berg.

ME AND "OLD BETSY"

III

The "Ya" Country

"You looking for something?" questioned a pioneer of a tall stalwart young man.

"I've found it." His light brown hair being pushed around by the breeze, his twinkly blue eyes ready to laugh, he did laugh as he added, "The Mississippi River."

"Well, there's a plenty of it there," rejoined the home-spun clad individual.

Carlos Ludwig von Berg was standing on the bank of the Mississippi at Moline.

Carlos had been there on the levee just looking. "Eye-balling" the river to which he had traveled so far to reach.

His expression was somewhat nostalgic, for the clear, wide river reminded him of his Rhine. He knew from his studies in Germany that this river was an artery as was the Rhine. Now he could see, too, that it was a line of demarkation. Where he stood was known country; across on the other side was mostly the unknown country.

Carlos had a good job back in New York. He was a German tutor for a prominent man's son.[1] His charge had asked him one day, "Carlos, let me see your tongue. Why! It's just like mine. My father said that you had a German tongue." This job was just until he could save enough money to start out for the West.

While in New York he had made a probable connection with the Hudson's Bay Company. They had given him a letter to one of their fur traders whom he might contact as a possible apprenticeship for a fur trader. He recalled with some chagrin, his inquiry as to this company, 'If it had anything to do with the Hudson River there?'

He was heading for McGregor, "Ioway"[2] as he found out that a number of his countrymen had settled throughout that area. There was even a settlement named Guttenberg close by McGregor. Furthermore, there was a possibility that this man, the fur trader, might be at McGregor.

Carlos had come this great distance to find out that Leipzig in his native land was the fur market of the world.

He hitchhiked a ride on a scow going upstream provided he would take his turn at the pole as well as help with loading and unloading at points on the river. Carlos was glad to have this chance to exert himself, as he was pent up with energy, so anxious was he to get into this new country.

The scow was loaded with homeseekers, their scant household belongings and livestock. He didn't know that this

---

(1)   Interview—St. Louis Post-Dispatch—Sunday Magazine, October 7, 1917.

(2)   Family Records and Letters furnished by his granddaughter, Miss Margaret A. Henry, Des Moines, Iowa.

was the original milk-run as the boat stopped at every town, settlement and any place in the wilderness, that would appeal to a new settler.

As the scow slowly made its way against the current, Carlos felt a warmth for the homespun appearance of the homesteads along the Mississippi. Their patches of fields seemed as if bartacked by the trees behind them and the houses of logs were closely notched for rugged wear.

His close contact because of the overcrowded condition of the craft engendered admiration for these dauntless homeseekers for with no assurance, simply fortitude and an inherent love for a home of their own, they faced the unknown.

A settlement above Moline, Le Claire, had no meaning to von Berg as the snub nose of the scow ran into the bank. In fact, its few settlers had about the same feeling, not knowing that years later it would be an historic spot. For it was where William Cody—Buffalo Bill—was born. Von Berg in after years heard of this spot from his close friend and scouting companion, Buffalo Bill, as they sat around campfires or huddled together without a fire because of the hostile Indians.

From Clinton, they "crept on" so it seemed to Carlos, to Dubuque. Here he was more than surprised at its size and bustle, for Dubuque showed the first sign of industry—the lead mines which had been discovered by the first white man to set foot in Iowa, 1785, a French-Canadian, Julian Dubuque.[3]

There was a girl on the scow, Bridget Bird. She was about Carlos's age. He was not interested in girls but he didn't mind talking to her as he made the sweep with the pole. Besides she was, he guessed, "on the pretty side". Her family was going to Beetown, Wisconsin.[4]

On the Wisconsin side they put in at Cassville. The

(3) Encyclopedia Britannica.

(4) Family Records & Letters furnished by his granddaughter, Miss Margaret A. Henry, Des Moines, Iowa.

only thing about Cassville to Carlos was that was where the Birds left the boat to go inland to Beetown. However, this little place later would be oft remembered by Bridget Mary and Carlos Ludwig.

Carlos's main interest was Indians. He saw his first Indians back at Chicago. He had a friendly feeling toward them right off. He admired their independent mien, their tall smooth bodies and their faces with no expressions. Only their eyes did all the expressing.

When they came to the confluence of the Wisconsin River, Carlos really got excited for he had been told that McGregor was just on ahead. When a shout came, "McGregor!" Carlos couldn't see anything but a bluff, then he saw that the settlement was between the bluff and the river. To be among his people was somewhat of a homecoming for Carlos. Too, he reverted to his native tongue. He was surprised at the size of McGregor. It was the postal center for that area with post roads[5] to other settlements, one of which went to Guttenberg. The fur trading there took most of Carlos's attention; he did notice that homesteaders up and down and across the river were there for supplies.

The fur trader to whom he had been directed had been at McGregor, but had moved on to Fort Snelling (St. Paul). Carlos decided that the scow was too slow so he bargained for a canoe and loading his equipment pushed off for Fort Snelling. To him this was his great adventure about which he had daydreamed from the time he left Germany. He paddled hard to leave the settlement of McGregor out of sight. That was in the summer of 1855 and that was the last ever seen of the young nobleman, von Berg. For like the tadpole which changes to a frog, Carlos metamorphosed into whatever it took in the wilderness of the "Ya" Country (as von Berg nicknamed it): Iowa on the left bank of the Mississippi, Wisconsin on the right bank and Minnesota above wherein were the headwaters of the Mississippi.

_____

(5)   Mrs. Lena D. Myers, Curator, McGregor Historical Museum, McGregor Library.

Passing some island and rounding a bend, the dip, dip of his paddle was the only audible sound. Ahead a kingfisher dipped into the Mississippi and instantly flew off carrying a fish in his beak. Over on the left bank he discerned several deer, the buck's head raised high, his antler prongs pointing skyward as he curiously watched the strange thing—canoe—in the water.

Carlos raised his eyes, he sat motionless, feeling the omnipotence of God.

When he arrived at Fort Snelling he found the fur trader to whom he had been directed. This man upon reading the letter, asked Carlos with whom he had come up from Mc-Gregor; and upon being told he had come by himself, the experienced fur trader grinned broadly as he said, "You're hired". Jack Frazier, half-breed was the veteran fur trader, one of the best with the Hudson's Bay Company.[6] In 1862, the year of the Sioux uprising, it was Jack Frazier who was invaluable as Indian scout for Colonel Henry H. Sibley.[7]

Carlos was briefed that their base was a factor at Fort Pembina at the confluence of the Pembina River and the Red River, located in the tip of the N.E. corner of North Dakota Territory, Canada just to the north and across the Red River was Minnesota.[8]

He informed von Berg that this factor was set up back in 1816 when John Jacob Astor (American Fur Company) had engineered the passage by Congress of an act restricting the issuance of fur trader's licenses to Americans.

Jack Frazier repeated the mandatory instruction from his company, 'To get along with the Indians.'

A Sioux Chief sitting on a log and being restrained in

---

(6)   Jack Frazier, being a half-breed, the conjecture is that he might have been the son of Robert Frazier, private with Lewis-Clark.

(7)   A History of Minnesota by William Watts Folwell, vol. II.

(8)   Hudson's Bay Company—letters—Mrs. Shirlee A. Smith, Librarian.

this position by a hand on each shoulder and these hands belonging to two standing braves, one on each side, needs clarifying.

The three were facing a teepee at the side of which stood a white hunter. This hunter had matured since we saw him leaving McGregor. He had filled out solidly with muscles. He stood arrow straight, clad in deer skin coat and pants and on his head was a beaver pelt cap. His blue eyes had narrowed somewhat giving him a gimlet-eyed squint. His face was set by his determined jaw and his skin was almost the tan of his clothes. Between his teeth he held a homemade paint brush and in his high hand was another. His attention was concentrated on two spots, one the sketch he was drawing on the skin of the teepee and the other the features of the Sioux Chief. His glance darted from one to the other as he painted.

Von Berg had started the portrait of this Indian Chief and almost with every stroke as he looked to his subject, the Indian Chief wasn't there, but had slipped behind him, eager to see how he looked. So after leading the Sioux back to the log and placing his head at the angle he wanted, von Berg returned to his canvas but after a few strokes his subject was missing and was breathing over his shoulder.

Von Berg cussed a little in Sioux but that didn't help. Finally, he had to resort to getting the two braves to hold his subject, somewhat like the early photographer had to use a metal brace to keep the head from moving as well as hold at the right angle.

Carlos was impervious to his surroundings—the pine forest of Minnesota and of the Indian village on the lake's edge.

In time he nodded and then motioned to the Chief to come take a look. The colors were sharp as were the features of the Chief. The portrait was fair but to the Chief it was miraculous. There was his likeness just as he had seen it, leaning over from his canoe into the crystal clear water of the lake.

Carlos took up painting among the Indians from necessity. All the traders had about the same trading goods—blankets, whisky (if a must), guns and on down to various trinkets. Many of the traders, especially the French-Canadians, had been in this territory long before he came and had the fur trade pretty well "sewed-up".

Having the latent desire to paint he tried this angle. He would depict, mostly on pieces of deer hide, animals and Indian symbols and with practice branched into portrait painting which required, in exchange, the Indians' finest furs and peltries.

He got along most friendly with the various tribes and could go from Sioux territory to Chippewa, Fox or Pawnee just as our modern salesmen go from city to city.

He knew their languages, supplemented with the universal sign language when necessary.

Carlos discovered the sterling character behind those high cheekboned redskins. He found them just like the whites, close knit families, honest and true friends.

He did not go along with Custer's statement, "that the only good Indian was a dead Indian".[9]

One experience was not what the Indian braves considered their standard but they overlooked his squawish attitude and showed appreciation for what he had done.

He was in an Indian village and one of the papooses was sick. The squaw mother did everything she could; the medicine man was called and he prescribed but still the little Indian baby cried continually and couldn't sleep.

Von Berg told the squaw mother to let him hold the papoose and he placed him on his shoulder and rocked back and forth in a sitting position as he sang the lullaby his mother had sung to him. The baby burped and presently went sound asleep. The squaw mother later sang along with

---

(9)   Life on the Plains or Personal Experiences with Indians, Gen. G. A. Custer, U. S. A.—Sheldon & Company.

von Berg until she got the tune of the lullaby; for to her it was the music that had been the quieter of her papoose.

Later the whites were astonished to hear the squaws of this tribe singing the "Lullaby" from *Erminie* with Indian words.

The various tribes returned Carlos's warmth of friendship. He entertained them around their camp fires with his "tall tales". The braves' "How! How! How!" resounded when he would imitate the French-Canadians in their speech. Then he would speak in the language of the English, and following this, with a "spiel" in his native tongue. This brought down the house.

Von Berg was a prowess at hunting, fishing and trapping, and he had companions in these fields in every tribe.

He enjoyed taking part in their games; and if he got a chance would pull some prank on one Indian much to the amusement of the others.

The Indians even counseled with him. Von Berg recalled a Medicine man of a Sioux tribe discussing with him his foreboding, which as he said wasn't like the sound of a buffalo herd or the sharp tattoos of deer running, but a distant sound coming from the East not like marching but a surge. He further confided to von Berg that he dare not lay it before his council for they would say right off that he was getting loco. Von Berg told him that his foreboding was correct, that his premonition was that of the white settlers coming, first a trickle that later would expand into a flood spreading over the vast land. The only thing for the Indians to do would be to move on to new lands or they would be driven out eventually.

"But let's just keep all this between us," von Berg advised. "You are riding your horse too fast," and he ended with a good natured laugh.

"The Indians taught me my geography lessons graphically by drawing on the ground with a stick the rivers and lakes. They showed me about a muddy river (Missouri) toward the west which meandered everywhere before it ran into the big river. This river (Minnesota) they pointed out goes to a fort (Fort Snelling). They located Spirit Lake and the rivers running west and east."

Von Berg had an affection for the North Star Country with its many lakes. He had canoed and portaged throughout its wilderness. His biggest thrill came when he viewed the big lake—Lake Superior.

"Many times," he related, "I felt that I was the first white man to paddle on those remote outstretches of water." But he went on to tell that he hadn't been in the fur business long until he found out that it wasn't the pioneer American whites who discovered this country but the fur traders made up of half-breeds, French-Canadians and others. These traders trickled into territories long before explorers moved in. Lewis-Clark on their memorable expedition met fur trader Charbonneau and his squaw wife, Sacajawea, at Fort Mandan.[10] Just as the explorers Fremont and Carson when they reached California—under Spanish regime—found fur traders there before them. The early fur traders, trappers and hunters were species of hardy, daring, cunning men. More like a pack of wolves, although they didn't always hunt in packs. But as with a wolf pack they fraternized as a group from necessity as they were pitted against Indian, English, French or Spanish domains. The peltries to them were as a pan of washed gold and no virtues stood in their way to obtain them. Floods, blizzards and other inclemencies might slow them up but that's all they did.[11]

Carlos liked the brass of the white settlers in this land of Northern Lights. At night—and they were long nights too—around their hearth, these rugged settlers became silver

(10) My life in the mountains and on the plains, by Davis Meriwether—University of Oklahoma Press. The Journals of Lewis and Clark —De Voto.

(11) Famous Frontiersmen—E. G. Cattermole A. B., courtesy of University of Oklahoma Library. The Reckless Breed of Men—Robert Glass Cleland.

tongued as to their harrowing experiences, deeds of bravery and tall yarns. In telling about this the "Old Scout" laughed heartily, "I guess some of this rubbed off on me".

It was a silent country and that's what appealed to Carlos.

"It was just like I was in a vacuum," he described it. This silence to some of the settlers, particularly the womenfolks, produced loneliness which in some cases brought on insanity. He recalled one instance when, ever alert to sounds, he heard soft steps approaching and, concealing himself waited. He didn't have long to wait for presently there appeared in the dense pine forest a lone white woman. She was out of her mind, having wandered away from her log cabin abode. She somewhat revived upon meeting a stranger and agreeably followed him as he took her to the nearest settlement. He felt that being with people would possibly restore her to normality.

At Mendota (proximity of Fort Snelling) he met a fur buyer for a rival company, The American Fur Company, H. H. Sibley[12] who later was the George Washington of Minnesota. He was Minnesota's first governor, and several years later, Commander-in-Chief of the troops who defeated the Sioux at Wood Lake.[13]

Carlos met many trappers and hunters and traders with whom in later years he was associated. One was Jack Crawford, famous border ranger,[14] rightly designated Poet Scout. This is one of his poems.[15]

---

(12)   Dominion of the North—Creighton, "Sibley knew the Sioux for he had traded among them since his arrival in the Minnesota area twenty-eight years before."

(13)   A History of Minnesota by William Watts Folwell.

(14)   Famous Frontiersmen—E. G. Cattermole A. B., courtesy of University of Oklahoma Library.

(15)   Echoes from the Mountains to the Plains by Major Wm. A. Bell, acknowledgment to Public Library of Denver and Yale University in making this rare booklet available.

SUNSHINE

I never like to see a man a-rastlin' with the dumps
'Cause in the game of life he doesn't catch the trumps;
But I can always cotton to a free and easy cuss
As he takes his dose, and thanks the Lord it isn't any wuss.
There ain't no use o'kickin' and swearin' at your luck,
Yer can't correct the trouble more'n you can drown a duck,
Remember, when beneath the load your sufferin'
    head is bowed,
That God'll sprinkle sunshine in the trail of every cloud.

If you should see a fellowman with trouble's flag unfurled,
An' lookin' like he didn't have a friend in all the world,
Go up an' slap him on the back an' holler "how d' you do?"
And grasp his hand so warm he'll know he has a friend in you.
Then ax him what's a-hurtin' 'im, and laugh his cares away,
And tell him that the darkest night is just before the day.
Don't talk in graveyard palaver, but say it right out loud,
That God'll sprinkle sunshine in the trail of every cloud.

This world at best is but a hash of pleasure and of pain,
Some days are bright and sunny, and some all sloshed
    with rain.
And that's just how it ought to be, for when the clouds roll by
We'll know just how to 'preciate the bright and smilin' sky.
So learn to take it as it comes, and don't sweat at the pores
Because the Lord's opinion doesn't coincide with yours,
But always keep rememberin', when cares your path enshroud
That God has lots of sunshine to spill behind the cloud.

    Carlos also trapped and hunted with James DeHaven
who was from McGregor[16] and later was an Indian scout
with Buffalo Bill.

---

    (16) Mrs. Lena D. Myers, Curator, McGregor Historical Museum,
McGregor Library.

Archie McIntosh was a co-worker with von Berg as he too was a fur trader with Hudson's Bay Company[17] and subsequently was a famous Indian scout.

Through "Ioway" on horseback over game trails von Berg sojourned taking in the western part. It was a hunter's paradise or as the Indians would put it, "Happy Hunting Grounds". The river bluffs were black with buffaloes when they made the crossing of the Missouri River. The beavers had made a dam across the Floyd River.[18] The Indians told of the terrible winter of '56-'57 which had wiped out more wildlife than all the tribes had killed.[19]

Sioux City was the fur trading center for as far west as the headwaters of the Missouri and up the Yellowstone. At Sioux City one firm's weekly receipts in 1857 were:[20]

7,567	buffalo hides (tanned)
739	beaver skins
32	elk skins
14	bear skins
1	moose skin
	etc.

Cash in this new country was hard to come by and what hard money the early settlers got was from the sale of their furs to fur traders such as von Berg. Not that Carlos carried his saddlebags loaded with money but he issued them a company promissory note which was the same as cash.[21]

"It was in this country that I was stalked by a panther, in fact, he was stalking both of us, my horse and me. My horse

(17) General George Crook, His Autobiography — Martin F. Schmitt, University of Oklahoma Press.

(18) History of the Counties of Woodbury and Plymouth, Iowa, A. Warner & Co. Publishers, 1890-91.

(19) Same as above.

(20) History of the Counties of Woodbury and Plymouth, Iowa, A. Warner & Co. Publishers 1890-91; "Messrs. Frost, Todd & Co."

(21) Hudson's Bay Company—letters, Mrs. Shirlee A. Smith, Librarian.

knew better than I did his vulnerability; like a dog he never left my side as I kept the campfire blazing. When I got a glimpse of two balls of fire in a tree, I let him have it. As we say at the bar, one drink calls for another, and that recalls another experience. I was hunting in the tall timber of Minnesota with a Fox Indian. It was getting dusk and we rode down the trail, canopied overhead with pine boughs. My Indian friend who was behind me fired his gun. To me it seemed that he was shooting at nothing until I heard a heavy thud not over two gallops ahead and there lay a large panther. I asked my lifesaver how he saw the panther for I wasn't any novice in the woods. He gave a sniffle meaning that he had smelled the cat. Then he told me that all he saw was a slight swing of the tree limb as the panther made ready to spring."

It was in that part of "Ioway" which later became Plymouth County that von Berg fancied the land. "I said to myself, I would like to settle in this country for it's level and will grow anything."

Von Berg chuckled in after years as he related about two creeks in that area, Big Whisky and Little Whisky. "When that country settled up, the womenfolks tried to change the names of these two creeks but it was a man's country and today they are Big Whisky and Little Whisky."[22]

Carlos saw the damage of the great Prairie Fire in the Spirit Lake region—a 10-15 mile strip seared to the bare earth.[23]

In "Ioway" von Berg contracted the "prairie digs",[24]

(22) History of the Counties of Woodbury and Plymouth, Iowa, A. Warner & Co. Publishers, 1890-91.

(23) History of the Counties of Woodbury and Plymouth, Iowa, A. Warner & Co. Publishers, 1890-91.
"The heavens were lighted up at night as though the whole globe was on fire and in the day time the smoke obscured the rays of the sun to such an extent as to leave the impression of deep twilight."

(24) History of the Counties of Woodbury and Plymouth, Iowa, A. Warner & Co. Publishers 1890-91

that pioneer scratching which went with the early life on the prairie.

Carlos looked forward to getting to Fort Dodge (Iowa) as here he got all the news from along the Mississippi River and beyond.

Every fall von Berg would join some tribe for their fall hunt. It was an occasion that he just couldn't miss. He lost his identity as a fur trader and was simply one of the tribe in their wild forage for winter meat and robes. After the bear hunting to deer hunting came the great sport of riding down the buffaloes in which the entire tribe took part. The strain was terrific but the sport offset it and as long as it was daylight the grand hunt went on.

At night around the campfires, after partaking of every kind of meat, they would live over the day's hunt and plan for tomorrow but before long the camp went dead as sleep followed a full stomach.

Every spring Carlos subconsciously was drawn back to McGregor. It wasn't the time to hunt, for wild life and wild Indians were preoccupied with what comes naturally. At these springtimes his mind became misty on hunting and his daydreams reverted back to that girl, Bridget, he had met on the scow when he first came to the wilderness. The trail led him back to his people. At the McGregor post he would always find a letter held for him from Bridget. After visiting with his countrymen in McGregor and the other German settlements he would make for Beetown. Out of curiosity, he said, to see if Bridget had married someone else. He wouldn't admit his relief when he found that she was still single.

So in the year 1861 in the month of May, he and Bridget Mary Bird were married at Cassville, Wisconsin,[25] and came back to McGregor[26] to make their home.

---

(25)   Department of the Interior, Bureau of Pensions.
(26)   Family Records & Letters furnished by his granddaughter, Miss Margaret A. Henry, Des Moines, Iowa.

He wrote to his family in Germany telling them that he was married and describing Bridget in many superlative adjectives.

Many months later presents came from the old country and among them was a very ornate cuckoo clock.[27] The little cuckoo had quite a musical tone and soon was a household pet. In this settlement on the Mississippi a cuckoo clock was a kind of clock very few had ever seen and many came to their home to hear and see this clock. The children loved it and although used to the rough and go of this pioneer country, behaved angelicly by the hours waiting for the bird to appear.

That fall, Carlos took leave of his bride. The urge for the Indians' fall hunt was in his blood. He decided to join up with the Sioux as they would hunt in the deep west in their Dakota territory. No sooner had he contacted the Sioux than his intuition told him something was different.

He was as welcome as he had always been but the undercurrent showed that they were keeping him under strict surveillance. "The eyes of the Sioux were upon him:" he was their prisoner.

He knew that the Sioux were disgruntled about their treaties not being lived up to by the white men; that their money from the U. S. Government was slower and slower in coming to them; and that the whites were encroaching on their Dakota lands due to gold being discovered there. Evidently, all this had built-up in some of the Sioux tribes to where they were going to take the situation into their own hands.

Carlos not only remembered but had been over the country where the Sioux went on the warpath in "Ioway"

---

(27) Mr. S. C. Dellinger, curator of museum of the University of Arkansas was given this clock by the family after Captain von Berg's death. It was in his home for a number of years until a neighbor boy attempted to climb the weight chain to catch the cuckoo.

back in 1857.[28] Their massacre had started below Sioux City and proceeded northeast along the Little Sioux River, scalping and killing as they went and burning everything which the settlers had built. Enroute they came to a settler's cabin. Mrs. E. Wilcox[29] appeared at the door with her children peeping out from around her skirts. Her husband was away, having gone to lay in supplies. This brave woman waved greetings to these war bedecked Sioux and instantly conveyed to them the question by signs, asking them if they were hungry? They were and Mrs. Wilcox brought out food for the Indians, making repeated trips to her cabin with the older children helping her. Mrs. Wilcox never showed any sign of fear but inwardly she was greatly alarmed that her husband might return and that would reverse the situation as, evidently, the Indians thought that she was a lonely widow woman left with all these children. The Indians ate the Wilcoxes "out of house and home" and then with friendly "Hows" went on their way north resuming their carnage. Not too far distant at Spirit Lake they massacred a settlement of about twenty.[30] This uprising faded out in the region of Spirit Lake. No reprisal on the Sioux was made, just a threat from Fort Dodge that the troops would hunt down the guilty tribes but that was as far as it went.

The Sioux knew that Carlos, the trader, would take back the information that the Sioux were preparing for the warpath if he was not kept as one of them in their tribe. Von Berg perceived the importance of escaping and warning the white settlers of the massacre in the making, but he also was aware that if he made a break he would be brought back before he could make good his escape.

Carlos von Berg related his dire predicament:[31]

---

(28)   Echoes from the Mountains to the Plains by Major Wm. A. Bell.

(29)   Same as above.

(30)   History of the Counties of Woodbury and Plymouth, Iowa, A. Warner & Co. Publishers, 1890-91.

(31)   Interview—St. Louis Post-Dispatch Sunday Magazine, Oct. 7, 1917.

"At the time of the annual hunt each tribe was the enemy of every other tribe and it was not unusual, when hostile hunting parties met, for them to abandon the chase and engage in battle.

"Three returning Sioux scouts reported a Pawnee hunting party on ahead and the Sioux decided upon a surprise attack at once. I was warned, on pain of death, not to attempt to escape during the battle. Some of the Indians forming a semi-circle escorted me and old Tusk-a-hoo, their medicine man, to a little hill overlooking where the Sioux expected to give battle to the Pawnees.

"Down the hill the rest of Little Crow's men then charged and presently the battle was on. Soon the fighters pressed nearer and nearer to where we were stationed. Men were falling on every side and wounded horses were plunging madly in clouds of dust. I trusted that my guards would forget me in the stress of the moment and lying flat on the neck of my faithful 'Pawnee Billy' I charged through the flying arrows into the valley half a mile below.

"There I paused to watch the fight to a finish and at dusk was joined by a handful of wounded Pawnees, all that was left of the hunting party. Little Crow and his victorious warriors had gone on their way down the far side of the hill.

"After helping the wounded Pawnees as much as I could, I left them and rode all night to get back so I could warn the settlers and the settlements of the impending uprising; and knowing Little Crow, I knew that he was equal to any deceit to carry out their plans.

"Some of the settlers made it to the Forts and others decided the Indians wouldn't dare start trouble. They didn't give the Indians credit for their acumen in feeling the pulse of the country: that the war between the whites was already taking many from the fields and settlements, and that even the whites were divided among themselves in these northern territories."

PRIVATE LOUIS VON BERG

(This picture taken years later at G.A.R. National Encampment)

IV

Company D 27th Regiment Iowa Infantry

"Private von Berg!"

"Yah."

"You are to report to Headquarters, immediately."

Headquarters were at Camp Franklin, Dubuque, Iowa.[1] Von Berg had enlisted as C. Louis von Berg anglicizing Ludwig and used the name Louis throughout his army service. After being mustered in at McGregor, August 20, 1862,

---

(1) Roster and Record of Iowa Soldiers in the War of the Rebellion, Vol. III Inter library loan: Carnegie-Stout Free Public Library, Dubuque, Iowa.

he was assigned to Co. D. 27th Regiment Iowa Infantry.[2]

This company of volunteers was made up mostly of German boys and a great many of them were foreign-born. Too, the majority was from Clayton County in which are McGregor, Guttenberg and Garnaville—all German settlements in the north east corner of Iowa.

At headquarters Louis was informed that he would leave immediately for Fort Snelling and report to Col. H. H. Sibley. These were his brief orders. Louis was still more puzzled to find that he was the only soldier being rushed to Fort Snelling.

As soon as he landed at Fort Snelling the news was everywhere that the Sioux had gone on the warpath.

Private von Berg muttered to himself, "That's not news; I told them it was going to happen a year ago."

Reporting to Col. Sibley he was ordered to look up Jack Frazier. Then the Colonel added with a quizzical smile, "Do you know him?"

Private von Berg tried to look serious as he replied, "Never heard of him," then he burst out laughing and the Colonel joined him.

Colonel Sibley then told von Berg that Jack Frazier had requested him. The two would do scout duty in locating the Sioux tribes. "They are holding as hostages many of our women and children."

"I know Lo, yah!" von Berg exclaimed. "I will go to him."[3]

When Frazier and von Berg met it was a warm reunion, while they made ready to leave. Louis was highly elated that his friend under whom he had served his apprenticeship of a fur trader had selected him to go on this dangerous mission.

(2)   Photocopy of Volunteer Enlistment.

(3)   Quoting Captain von Berg from Sunday Magazine—St. Louis Post-Dispatch—October 7, 1917.
"Lo" is a proper name.

Jack briefed Louis on what had happened. Aug. 18, 1862, the Sioux led by Chief Little Crow—"the biggest little redskin devil that ever wore a war bonnet and a Government blanket"[4]—went on the warpath. Their first surprise attack was just below the mouth of Redwood River. They pillaged, scalped and murdered at every clearing and settlement. The settlers who escaped reached Fort Ridgely. At the Redwood River Ferry the whites made a stand but were outnumbered and outsmarted by the Sioux.

Fort Ridgely was undermanned. Although the settlers pouring in did add some fighting strength to the garrison, at the same time it increased their liability because of the added number of women and children.

Chief Little Crow planned his strategy well. The Sioux would take Fort Ridgely; then on to New Ulm and from there they could easily ravage the country to Fort Snelling. Too, they would take some women and children as hostages, which would be top priority trading goods with the whites.

Fort Ridgely had been an ordnance fort earlier and some cannons had been left behind. Sergeant Jones who was at Fort Ridgely had been attached to this artillery. He conscripted some of the defenders to man these cannons, not knowing whether the old cannons would function or explode.

The Sioux attacked with confidence as they greatly outnumbered the garrison. The Minnesota boys repulsed their first attack. However, on their second attack the Sioux succeeded in getting to some of the buildings which had served as outer fortifications. As the Indians swarmed in for the kill, Sergeant Jones gave the order to fire the cannons. The old cannons and green crews synchronized perfectly. The volley caused consternation among the Indians as gaps were torn through their charging braves. The cannon balls were a mode of warfare the Sioux had not expected. The Indians withdrew, at what they thought was a safe distance. After a pow-

---

(4) Said by Major William A. Bell quoted from Sunday Magazine —St. Louis Post-Dispatch—October 7, 1917.

wow they circled and came in from the opposite direction. But they found that those wagon guns could be turned around and again they couldn't take it, that of seeing ponies and riders wiped out as though they hadn't even been there. This time when the Sioux drew back they evidently decided they would by-pass Fort Ridgely and go on to New Ulm as that is what they did.

New Ulm had received some reinforcements. The Sioux arrived at New Ulm and strutted their array of war bonnets and war ponies. Their first attack was somewhat premature as all their forces had not come up. It was repulsed. The Sioux drew back and waited, evidently for Chief Little Crow (who had been wounded at Fort Ridgely) to join them. Then they spearheaded their second attack. No doubt their defeat at Fort Ridgely and the repulse of their first attack on New Ulm dampened the Sioux's fire—the rain helped, too—for valiantly the outnumbered whites repulsed them a second time.

The Sioux then changed their sight from Fort Snelling and headed in a northwestern direction, devastating as they went and taking captive women and children.[5]

The second governor of Iowa, Alexander Ramsey, called out the state militia. He made an urgent call for volunteers to assemble at Fort Snelling. He also sent a dispatch to the U. S. Government asking for reinforcements. He did not know whether it was the entire Sioux Nation on the warpath or just some of the Sioux tribes incited by Chief Little Crow. He appointed his political adversary, Col. Henry H. Sibley as Commander-in-Chief.

The homesteaders rallied to protect their families and homes as the young men had been siphoned off for the Civil War.[5]

Col. Sibley had called on Jack Frazier to be his scout;[5]

---

(5) A History of Minnesota—William Watts Folwell. The Sioux Uprising of 1862—Kenneth Carley. The Minnesota Historical Society inter library loan, courtesy of Arkansas Library Commission, Little Rock, Ark., Miss Freddy Schader.

Jack had requested the help of Louis von Berg; as he stated the two of them knew the Sioux and the Sioux country best and where one might fail to come back the other might make it.

Louis told Frazier about his escapade last fall with the Sioux.

While Col. Sibley was moving some forces up the river to St. Peter so as to allay New Ulm and Fort Ridgely, Jack and Louis took up the trail of the Sioux. From the direction of the trail they surmised that the Sioux were making for their favorite campground in the Wood Lake area. It took their combined skill in woodcraft to slip by the Sioux lookout braves. To the consternation of the Sioux these two brave scouts walked into their camp and in Sioux language demanded that they be taken to Chief Little Crow's teepee.

Little Crow was cordial to his old friends and after a pipe of peace they counseled. Jack and Louis were relieved to find out that it was not the entire Sioux Nation they were up against but some disgruntled tribes headed by Chief Little Crow and other lesser chiefs.

Chief Little Crow, a treacherous fighter and councilman, demanded that the whites move back to the Mississippi River and, if not, the Sioux would kill every woman and child they held as hostage.

Jack and Louis, not the least bit scared by his threat, told him that they would carry his message back to their Chief, and warned him that the whites could also kill Indian squaws and children and war ponies.

The scouts asked Chief Little Crow for an escort back to their lookout line so as to rush his message to their White Chief.

When Frazier and von Berg reached St. Peter and conferred with Colonel Sibley, the three agreed that the only thing to do was to advance on the Sioux "at once if not sooner".

Alarming reports had come in of attacks even across the Missouri River into Dakota Territory and into various settlements to the north in Meeker County, Iowa.

Up the Minnesota River Col. Sibley led his forces. Of course, the Sioux knew of their movements and planned an ambush. When that was dicovered by what was left of the Third Minnesota, the Sioux were mauled by the revengeful whites and surrendered at Wood Lake. That was in the latter part of September, 1862.[5]

The rescuing of the white hostages and the reunion of some of the families was a most joyous time. The Sioux had their prisoners-of-war camp up the river and it was named later Camp Release (Montevideo).[5]

Although the Sioux were punished for this uprising, it was significant in that it was the spark that ignited the Sioux Wars which lasted until 1891.

At Camp Franklin orders were received by Col. James I. Gilbert, Commanding Officer of the 27th Regiment—Oct. 17, 1862—to embark his regiment to Fort Snelling in case Col. Sibley needed reinforcements.[6]

After arriving at Fort Snelling, Col. Gilbert received orders to march six companies from Fort Snelling to Mille Lacs area—125 mile hike—for the purpose of superintending the payments of annuities to the friendly Indians in that section of the state. The main purpose however was to impress the Indians with this array of military strength.[7]

Von Berg's scouting work completed, he rejoined his company at Fort Snelling and was made a Corporal.

From there the regiment embarked to Cairo, Illinois which was the depot for war operations in the western theatre.[8]

---

(6)   Roster and Record of Iowa Soldiers.

(7)   Same as above.

(8)   Same as above.

"Look how wide the four-eyed so-and-so is," commented one of the boys in Blue.

"Not clear either like it is at McGregor," added another.

From Cairo, the 27th embarked to Memphis, Nov. 20, 1862 and were integrated into General Grant's army.[9]

The 27th Iowa Regiment fought the Civil War from the time of induction to mustering out, in the main, on the Mississippi River and it tributaries.

Corporal von Berg in writing home said, "Why, they are calling us river rats."

Their first engagement was on the Tallahatchie River below Waterford, Miss.; then up the Mississippi to Memphis.[10]

Leaving Memphis they landed on the other bank of the Mississippi at Helena, Ark.

Louis von Berg was detailed from Aug.-Oct., 1863 to Battery A 3 Ill. Arty. Regt.[11] This battery was with General Steele in the occupation of Little Rock on the Arkansas River.

His old regiment, the 27th Iowa, was there as part of the Army of Arkansas but was held in reserve.[12]

Sept. 29, 1863 Corporal von Berg requested to be reduced back to a private, no reason given, request granted.[13] Louis was mustered in as a private and was mustered out as one.

Nov. 15, 1863, from Little Rock the 27th went to DeValls Bluff, Ark. on the White River and embarked down the river to the Mississippi.[14] The 27th boys liked the White

---

(9)   Roster and Record of Iowa Soldiers.

(10) Same as above.

(11) Photocopy, Company Muster Roll, July and August, 1863.

(12) Roster and Record of Iowa Soldiers.

(13) Photocopy, Company Muster Roll, September and October, 1863.

(14) Roster and Record of Iowa Soldiers.

River catfish. Had to get an old darky to show 'em how to catch 'em.

Up and down the Mississippi they shuttled—Memphis, Vicksburg, Meridian, Greenville.

Jan. 28, 1864, the boys of the 27th had an itch two ways—itching to get at the enemy and scurvy. Their record thus far was one for the book, having been in service 15 months and having no direct contact with enemy, yet suffering losses of 25%.[15]

The 27th got their baptism with real fire during the Red River Campaign. The Red River Campaign was all but a disaster for General Banks. The reason it was not was the 27th Iowa. At Marksville, on the Red River the 27th was placed on rear guard duty. The boys of the 27th fought like they were advancing rather than covering almost a riot re-treat. One soldier in Gray (who was taken prisoner) was overheard telling about it, "We had those damnyankees on the run, more ways than a country boy can whip a mule. Had 'em jumping in bayous like catfish on the line. Then up jumped a rear guard of jabbering Germans who evidently didn't understand English and like boll weevils they came, running us back to our artillery."

General Banks said of the 27th Iowa, "You have saved the army," and coming from a defeated general, it was the whole truth.[16] The Iowa Roster and Record said about him, "Red River Expedition—through the utter incapacity of the Commanding General Nathaniel P. Banks".

August, 1864 returning from Oxford, Miss. to Memphis, stoppage was entered against von Berg for waist belt and plate, one cap, pouch and one bayonet.[17] His buddies carried him high about these purchases and many a gibe they made at him but all they could get out of Louis was a grin and "Dogwatch".

---

(15)   Roster and Record of Iowa Soldiers.

(16)   Same as above.

(17)   Photocopy, Company Muster Roll, July and August, 1864.

Back to Cairo, then St. Louis and Jefferson Barracks. Here they contacted some of the "Ioway" boys from 18th, 19th, 20th Regiments who had been in the Battles of Pea Ridge and Prairie Grove. From them they heard about the Ozarks in S. W. Missouri and N. W. Arkansas which gave them such a bad time in the rain and snow.[18]

This time they left the Mississippi and marched across Missouri to the Kansas Border in pursuit of General Sterling Price. [19]

Von Berg in telling about this trek said, "We had a boy in our company whose name was Beilharz and he never let us forget the Mississippi. He could cup his hands and make a loud sound just like a steamboat whistle. Every time we would cross, even just a jumping creek, old Beilharz would let out his steamboat whistle."

The 27th got back to St. Louis and the Mississippi River, Nov. 18, 1864.[20]

Their next river was up the Ohio to the Cumberland River and then up this river although it was going down south, to Nashville. Later they marched over to Clifton on the Tennessee River, another tributary of the Mississippi, then down the Tennessee to the Ohio and from there to the unpredictable river—the Mississippi.[21]

Private von Berg had no room in his haversack for canvas, paints and brushes; but he did have time to carve a cane. On the end of the crook he carved an eagle's head. On the prong which stuck out about midway he carved a deer's head. The tip of the cane was a metal shell case. He painted on the cane the two companies he was with, the 27th Iowa and the 3rd Illinois Arty, also a shield insignia of the American flag. Then up and down the cane was a design of stems and leaves.

(18)   The Diary of an Unknown Soldier.
(19)   Roster and Record of Iowa Soldiers.
(20)   Same as above.
(21)   Same as above.

His work was meticulously done and required patience and many hours.[22]

It was at Eastport, Miss., that Louis von Berg was granted a 30 day furlough beginning Feb. 1, 1865, so he could go home as he had received word that his wife and only child were desperately ill.[23]

While Louis was on his furlough his regiment took a river steamer to Cairo on Feb. 9, 1865.[24]

Louis was to rejoin his company there March 2, 1865.

When he reported on Feb. 28, 1865, his regiment had gone, having received hurry-up orders Feb. 21, 1865, to go by boat to New Orleans.[25]

So. Louis von Berg was "absent without leave".

March 7, 1865, his regiment shipped out from New Orleans on the ocean steamship, Empire City, for Dauphin Island, Alabama.[26]

Louis caught up with his regiment at Dauphin Island, March 12, 1865. How he made such record time from Feb. 28 to March 12 from Cairo, Ill., to Dauphin Island, Alabama, there is no record.

His commanding officer wrote the following in Louis's behalf:

Head Quarters Co. D 27th Regt.
Iowa Vol. Inf.
Dauphin Island, Ala., March 13th. 1865

Sir

I would most respectfully ask you, to restore Louis von Berg, a Private of my Company, to his pay, as he has been

---

(22) This cane is in the University of Oklahoma Museum, Norman, Oklahoma.

(23) Photocopy, Company Muster Roll, January and February, 1865.

(24) Roster and Record of Iowa Soldiers.

(25) Same as above.

(26) Same as above.

reported on my Company Returns, "absent without leave" from March 3d to March the 11th/65/both dates incl. The said Private Louis von Berg received at Eastport Mips. a furlough for 30 days, to commence February the 1st. 1865 and to expired March the 2nd. 1865.—He reported at Cairo Ill. on the 28th day of February 1865, (as per statement affixed to his furlough, which is in my possession)—and it was only owing to the removal of our Army Corps to the Department of the Gulf, that said soldier failed, to return to his Company at the proper time.—He reported to me on the 12th. day of March 1865 and I therefore recommend him earnestly to be restored to his rights without any loss or punishment whatever.

I am Sir

Very Respectfully
Your most obedient servant

Alexander Bliedung
1st. lt. & Comdg. Co. D 27th Iowa

To
    I. B. Sample
Maj. & A. A. G.
    2d. Divis. 16th A C[27]

This trip on the lower Mississippi completed Louis' survey of his American Rhine. Here he was at the mouth of the Mississippi and a long time ago it seemed to him now, he had stood at Lake Itasco, the headwaters of the Mississippi. He noticed the difficulty encountered with bars formed from the sediment, and it required constant dredging to enable ships to clear the mouth and enter the gulf. Too, the sediment from the Mississippi left its mark far out into the gulf.

April 3, 1865 the 27th was again under General Steele at the siege of Fort Blakely, Alabama.[28]

---

(27)   Photocopy of letter.

(28)   Roster and Record of Iowa Soldiers.

April 9 was an indelible binary date, one of which the 27th found out later:

> Fort Blakely was captured,
> General Lee surrendered.

July 14, 1865 orders came to proceed to Vicksburg, Miss. and then report to commanding officer for muster out and discharge from service.[29]

From Vicksburg the 27th. Iowa embarked on steamer, "Commonwealth" for St. Louis.

Everyone was asking everyone else, "What are you going to do when you are mustered out?"

Beilharz remarked dryly, "I'm going to get rid of my webfeet".

At St. Louis they transferred to the steamer, "Canada" and arrived at Clinton, Iowa, Aug. 2, 1865.

Quote from The Clinton Herald, Aug. 5, 1865:

The 27th Iowa Infantry, in command of Lieut. Col. Judd Lake, arrived here about half-past twelve o'clock Wednesday noon, on board the steamer, Canada, and as its arrival had not been preannounced, no preparation whatever had been made for its reception. Indeed the 1st. knowledge that many of our citizens had of the presence of more soldiers was upon hearing the enlivening strains of the brass band which accompanied the regiment, and which preceded it in its march to camp. The facts, however, no sooner reached the ears of the ladies, than active preparations were at once commenced for giving the soldiers the customary "square meal," but here not a little difficulty was experienced as the larders seemed to be unusually destitute of cakes and other delicacies, and there was not time to be lost in making them. Nevertheless, a bountiful repast was soon spread upon the tables in the grove, and the cheerful faces and willing hands of the ladies present made up for anything

---

(29) Roster and Record of Iowa Soldiers.

lacking in quantity or quality of the food. We speak by the card when we assure the ladies that their patriotic efforts in behalf of the soldiers are fully appreciated and will never be forgotten.[30]

Quote from The Clinton Herald for Saturday, August 12, 1865:

The 27th Infantry, Col. Judd Lake, was mustered out and paid off on 8/8/65. No better regiment ever went into service, and the conduct of its members while here showed them to be good citizens as well as brave soldiers. The officers labored diligently on muster rolls and pay rolls and promptly did their duty. The men were quiet and unobtrusive, proving that they were well disciplined and reflecting great credit upon their officers as well as themselves by a gentlemanly deportment that has not been excelled.[30]

1st. Lt. Comdy. Co D 27th Iowa, Alexander Bliedung wrote the following about Louis von Berg:

"As I can represent said soldier as a brave and prompt soldier who has been with his company since its original organization and who was present in all the engagements and on all the campaigns in which the Regiment and Company was."[31]

(30)   Courtesy of Free Public Library, Clinton, Iowa.
(31)   Photocopy of letter.

V

"Them Wolves Are Indians"

Well-nigh 12 years after Louis von Berg stood on the east bank of the Mississippi, he was again standing on the east bank of a river but this time it was "Big Muddy" (Missouri) near Sioux City. Parenthetically, he had Americanized his name to Charles von Berg.

Where he stood was known country; where his gaze and heart were concentrated was far into the distance on the other side—Sioux Lands—the Dakota Territory.

Charles was just as exuberant and vibrant as he was when he first saw the Mississippi, but his visage now was hard and rather stoical.

"Curley"
Painted by Captain Charles L. von Berg

He drank deep of the panorama. Then he whistled for his horse which was grazing at large, mounted and headed north. He was going up into Plymouth County which was just above Woodbury County in which was the land office at Sioux City.

When Charles Louis von Berg returned to his family at McGregor after being mustered out, and the honeymoon following the war had ended, the question came up, and from his wife, "What do you plan to do?" It started off as husband and wife pillow talk but it ended in a brawl of words. "You have your family to think about now. You owe it to our boy to get into some respectable occupation." Finally, "I'm going to take Little Charlie and go home to Beetown if you go back into that fur trading stink".

Napoleon had his Waterloo, and so did Charles von Berg —at Waterloo, Iowa.[1] He found a "respectable occupation" as half owner in a general store there, and that's where the family lived shortly after the war. As the business cycle right after a war is generally not so good, their business was no exception during those hard times. Charlie (Charlie Berg for short with most of his friends) was enthusiastic about adding buying and selling peltries in their store. "Why, we can make two profits. One on the hides and another on our supplies we trade them in exchange for their furs." However, smelly peltries didn't exactly go along with groceries any more than did coal oil sloshed over on potatoes. Nor was Charlie Berg cut of the pattern to be a storekeeper, so in time, he got out of the store.

"I'll tell you what I'll do, Mary. Remember my telling you about that rich land over above Sioux City. Yah! I will ride over there and homestead us some of that land. My time in the army will apply on my homestead.[2] I'll build us

_____

(1) Letter from his granddaughter, Miss Margaret A. Henry, Des Moines, Iowa.

(2) Homestead Act of Congress 1862. History of the Counties of Woodbury and Plymouth, Iowa.

a house and then you and Little Charlie," von Berg stopped and smiled anticipatively, "can come out."

Charles followed the Floyd River into Plymouth County. He was amazed, for when he had last seen this country it was a "hunter's paradise." Now it was dotted with settlers' homes, surrounded with fields of corn and wheat. Too, he found a little town had been started there. It was named Le Mars. He was quite pleased with himself that he had picked out this area years ago as being some of the richest land in Iowa.

Out from Le Mars about five miles he located his homestead and staked out 181.78 acres. Returning to Sioux City, Charles von Berg went to the Land Office and registered his homestead.[3]

Later at the bar of the Terrific Hotel[4] he met some of his fur trading "pardners." It was a drink-'em-up reunion. He announced to them that he was through with fur trading. That from here out he was going to smell like a farmer instead of a skunky fur trader.

One of his friends "took the floor." "Somebody out here said, 'Nothing is stronger than the pioneer instinct and many of those white men who were just behind the Indians and the buffaloes here, are yet at their heels still farther on toward the setting sun.'[5] That's us. I'll make a wager, Charlie Berg. That you will too."

Back to his homestead Charlie von Berg returned. With help from his good neighbors, Charlie built his home. All the timber for the von Berg house was cut from his own land. One of the earliest settlers was Jacob Rubel who said he was the second homesteader in that area.[6]

---

(3) Homestead Certificate No. 655.

(4) "Terrific" name of early hotel in Sioux City, History of the Counties of Woodbury and Plymouth, Iowa.

(5) Page 410, History of the Counties of Woodbury and Plymouth, Iowa.

(6) Page 493, History of the Counties of Woodbury and Plymouth, Iowa.

Von Berg had time, too, for his hunting and fishing. On one trip to Sioux City he ran into some rich boys from the East wanting a guide to hunt buffaloes. This trip was so successful that it gave Charlie the idea, he could be guide to hunters in the wintertime and a farmer during the growing and harvest season.

Charles received a letter which he proudly showed around Le Mars, announcing that his wife and boy were on their way.

Mrs. von Berg liked everything about their new home, particularly the rich land, and her remark was, "This is where I am going to live and die."[7] Little Charles, who was seven now, liked it too. His father had a present for him, a boy's size Indian bow and arrows.

Charlie von Berg received word from Sioux City that nobility from England were coming to Sioux City. They wanted a guide for a deluxe buffalo hunt in the vicinity of Fort McPherson. It was Lord Dunraven's first trip. At Fort McPherson, Charlie met his old friend, Charley Reynolds who introduced him to a younger scout and hunter, Buffalo Bill. Von Berg and Buffalo Bill took to each other mainly because they looked enough alike to be twins. Von Berg asked Buffalo Bill where he had got his name. Buffalo Bill told him that he had been the buffalo hunter for the railroad gang building the Kansas Pacific. He introduced Charlie von Berg to Dr. Frank Powell, "White Beaver," who was the contract surgeon at Fort McPherson.[8]

The three hit it off as old time buddies as not one of them could outdrink the others. Lonesome Charley (Charley Reynolds) never joined them in this part of the hunt.

Von Berg didn't like what he heard about the Indian trouble down in Kansas. "It could be like a prairie fire," he brooded.

---

(7)   And she did. (Died, May 1913 at Le Mars.)

(8)   The Lives and Legends of Buffalo Bill—Don Russell.

"Wild Bill (Hickok) is scouting down there," Buffalo Bill told him.

They told Charlie about Major Forsyth's gallant fight on Beecher's Island. The three had a good laugh which called for another drink, when Buffalo Bill related what one of the "toughies" (they were mostly inveterate scouts) with Major Forsyth said, "If you want to love a color, just get saved by it once."[9] He was referring to their rescue by the boys in Blue from Fort Wallace.

Later von Berg was guide and hunter to other English nobility, Lord Fenton in particular. Many years later in the von Berg collection of Western and Indian mementoes and his collection of his own paintings there were two pieces which were entirely incongruous. One was an English riding whip and the other a small fox horn, both of which had been given to him by Lord Fenton.[10] Von Berg was justly proud of the fox horn for it was a personal piece which carried the coat of arms of the Fentons and had been in that family for two centuries.

Von Berg was one of the scouts and hunters for the plush hunt complimentary to the Grand Duke Alexis of Russia in 1872 under the auspices of the United States Government.[11] General Sheridan had personal charge assisted by many other "top brass." Custer was one and Major Forsyth, still limping from his harrowing experience on the Arickaree Fork, was another. North Platte—Nebraskaland—was the getting off place for the Grand Duke's hunting party.

---

(9)   Buffalo Land—W. E. Webb.

(10)   Echoes from the Mountains to the Plains—1907—Major Wm. A. Bell.
also
Quoting from tape recording made by Ward Mayes, Meridian, Idaho referring to Captain von Berg's collection, "Scouted (guide) for nobility for English especially. Leashes that they kept the dogs tied and all their hunting supplies and everything and he had these also."

(11)   Personal Interview: Sunday Magazine—St. Louis Post-Dispatch, October 7, 1917.

Buffalo Bill put on his first Wild West Show for the Grand Duke as he directed Chief Spotted Tail and his warriors in an Indian buffalo hunt;[12] and this was followed that night by a pageant of an Indian war dance.

Ever after that hunt, von Berg would joshingly tell his hunters to whom he was guide, "Now, there won't be any carpets in the tents like it was for Grand Duke Alexis."

Springtime found Charlie Berg back on his farm at Le Mars with his wife, Little Charlie and Albert—"kleiner Bub," born 1869. Big Charlie was no better at farming than he had been as a storekeeper. This wasn't altogether his fault as one season he went through a drought. Another, when it looked like he "had it made," the grasshoppers harvested his crops.[13]

So Charlie had to get work until next planting time. He took a job with the railroad[14] which was booming now that the transcontinental railroad had been completed. His railroad connection brought to his attention the two volumes, *New Tracks in North America,* by Dr. William Abraham Bell, which told of Bell's exploits while with the surveying team for the Kansas Pacific.[15]

These volumes helped Charlie Berg reassure himself, even though he didn't convince his wife, that his future was in the West.[16]

In the issue of June 14, 1873, *The Rocky Mountain News* in Denver carried a list of letters uncalled for at the post office and on this list was one for "C. von Berg."[17]

---

(12)   The Lives and Legends of Buffalo Bill—Don Russell.

(13)   Letter from his granddaughter, Miss Margaret A. Henry, Des Moines, Iowa.

(14)   Mason City, Iowa.

(15)   Published in London, 1869, Chapman and Hall; Later Dr. Bell was associated with General William Jackson Palmer on the Denver and Rio Grande Railroad.

(16)   "Pioneers are born not made." History of the Counties of Woodbury and Plymouth, Iowa.

(17)   Courtesy The Public Library, The City and County of Denver, Western History Department.

Today in that city in the Public Library, Western History Department, are two painting on trays signed by Charles L. von Berg.[18]

Another memento of his from the Rocky Mountains is the flower collection made from the wild flowers there. One of his kin, a favorite niece, Mrs. Joe Flanagan,[19] who liked to draw and did so under his encouragement at his desk— made of heavy cherry and walnut, put together with wooden pegs, with a slanting top on hinges and compartment underneath[20]—said of this collection, "It is as delicate as a fine piece of embroidery." And she marveled that a rough Indian fighter had the patience and the delicate touch to assemble such a collection.

1873, von Berg was scout under General David Sloane Stanley when he led his expedition into the Yellowstone area[21]—Custer was on this expedtition too—against Rain-in-the-face. In the von Berg collection is a pipe of peace given him at one time by Rain-in-the-face. General Stanley had this to say about von Berg in his "Personal Memoirs": "Captain von Berg was reliable and nonexcitable and whenever he came to me with information, it was dependable."

Charlie Berg was back from the West—having come home to bring his children their school lunch money—when Charley Reynolds came up the Missouri as scout for General Custer on his exploratory trip into the Black Hills.

---

(18) Quoting from letter June 22, 1965. The Public Library, The City and County of Denver, Mrs. Alys Freeze, Head, Western History Department: "Among our pictures are two 12-inch metal trays painted in oil by von Berg. One is identified around the rim of the tray by the artist as 'Up in Ozark Mountain, 1906.' The other as 'Col. W. F. Cody's mountain home foots of Yellowstone Park on the Shoshone River Range. TE 1906', inscribed to Wm. Bell."

(19) Her maiden name was Ruth Mayes. Was related to Captain von Berg's second wife, Mrs. Martha Louisa von Berg.

(20) Captain von Berg's desk was a gift to the writer from Bob, his wife Peaches and their son, Marlin Mayes, relatives of Captain von Berg's second wife.

(21) Dictionary of American Biography.

Von Berg jokingly said to Reynolds, "If you find any gold up there in those Black Hills let me know." Although von Berg was jocular about it, he knew that there had been trickles of information coming out of the Black Hills about gold being there. He also observed that in Custer's forces were competent miners, which spelled out that it was far from a goodwill expedition among the Sioux.

That same year, 1874, von Berg had this escapade when he was with Colonel Mackenzie in the Texas Panhandle. "We suddenly, after following what I thought was a small band of Indians, found ourselves virtually pinned down by sheer number of Kiowas on war ponies. I was very much chagrined for I had permitted the detachment to fall for an old Indian trick—that of following a pell mell retreat of the Indians until we topped the rise; it wasn't a retreat after all but a guise to lure us into a trap. (The Japs used this old trick, too, in the Pacific.) I'll tell you later how the Sioux used this strategy on General Crook at the Battle of the Rosebud. Yah! I gave an instant recommendation to Colonel Mackenzie. Have your men count off. The odd numbers shoot at the riders. The even numbers shoot at their war ponies . This is no tall tale; the Indians would rather die in battle than to lose their mounts—war ponies—which were their greatest love. The Colonel issued the order. As the Indians rode in a little closer, the volley from our boys took a different toll. The Indians' ponies went down, blocking the fast riding warriors behind them. Further volleys from our Cavalry created further chaos. There was a barricade of horseflesh—immobile—and scrambling Indians who were easily picked off. It was a bad omen to the Indians. They pulled back, salvaging as many of their wounded and dead as they could. This gave our 'men in leather' a chance to back out of the trap. This we did on the double, never slackening reins until we had the main body of our army in sight."[22]

---

(22)   Arkansas Gazette, Sunday, Nov. 1, 1964, Feature Story.

Later in the Panhandle Campaign, Colonel Mackenzie led his cavalry down the canyon wall of the Palo Duro on just a narrow game trail—an almost unbelievable feat—and surprised and routed the Kiowas.

Explaining an exhibit in his collection, that of a horse's tail, Captain von Berg first displayed one of his paintings. It was of his famous scouting horse, "Pawnee Billy." "We were up in Montana, me and 'Pawnee Billy.' A trooper was with me. Together we were scouting to locate the main body of the Sioux. It was in rather open country with brush about head high. We hadn't seen any tracks of Sioux nor had I got a whiff of the vermin. I heard the whine of the arrow as it pierced 'Pawnee Billy', through the crest of his neck. The arrowhead sticking out one side of his neck and the feathers the other. That arrow was intended for me, his lead was just a little too much. It came home to me then, how the Indians felt about losing their war ponies. I and 'Old Betsy' went into automatic action. I fired four shots. Wondered why my trooper buddie hadn't fired. When I glanced toward him, I knew. They are good Sioux now," grinned von Berg as he pointed out four Indian scalps which were tied together by the characteristic Sioux topknots."[23]

Charles von Berg painted several pictures of camp life depicting his scouts in the mountains and Bad Lands. One of these show several scouts making camp in a dense forest below a high bluff on the top of which is an Indian crouched holding his gun. This is one of the best paintings[24] and has a significant story.

One of the scouts had brought in a point deer and laid it down by a stump. The scouts had cut the tree down for firewood. One of the scouts is probably getting the coffee ready before the blazing campfire around the log. Charlie Berg and the scout—who had brought in the deer—

---

(23)   Sunday Magazine—St. Louis Post-Dispatch—Oct. 7, 1917 and Echoes from the Mountains to the Plains—1907.

(24)   Picture in the room of his great-grandson, Emmetsburg, Iowa.

are standing back apparently giving advice as to the coffee making; but in reality the other scout is confiding in Charlie that when he came back to camp with his deer, he espied an Indian on top of the high bluff overlooking their camp.

Charlie Berg told him that he would slip out through the thick woods, which are most naturally depicted, showing pine or fir together with oak. The giants of the forest reaching into the sky form an irregular line of foliage tops.

The three horses around the camp, from their demeanor, show that they have had it—a hard day's ride.

While the other scouts continued the preparation for their evening meal, Charlie Berg left the camp in the opposite direction of the rock ledge to circle around and come in at the back of the cliff.

In the painting the Indian peering over the rocks with the sky as background projecting him in relief is marvelous —almost portraitlike.

The grass on top of the bluff is lush in that one foot of the Indian's is ankle deep in it. Nature and erosion and time had sculptured on this bluff—with the grass as his hair, below this a crevice forming the eyes, a prominence beneath this the nose and below this another crevice, the mouth— the head of a ferocious Indian.

Von Berg, catlike, made his way up the precipice and completely surprised the Indian, whose instinct must have told him of danger. For he glanced behind him and saw "Eagletail" with his gun ready to shoot. This glance behind saved the Indian's life for von Berg recognized him. He was a former hunting companion who had saved "Eagletail's" life. This Indian had shot a cougar which was in the act of making a spring. The two had a friendship powwow and the scout returned to camp. "I had to tell a white lie," von Berg chuckled, "I told them that when I got up there the Indian had already slipped away."

Whether the next experience happened with this same

band of scouts is immaterial. We'll let the Captain tell it. He was questioned about a bloodstain on the sleeve of his buckskin jacket. "That had to do with a love story. Yah!" and his eyes twinkled. "Your history books say the frontiersmen hold that the only good Indian was a dead Indian. They tell us also that the Sioux were a bloodthirsty people who took delight in lifting scalps regardless whether they were of men, women or children; that they had no feeling and were always cruel even among their own people. Just about the opposite is true. For I have seen the tenderness of a brave for his papoose or squaw. Their squaws were true to their mates, truer than some of us today.

"Take this stain now. That came from an incident during the war with the Sioux. I had been sent to scout the location of their forces. Five of us were together. We usually scouted with fewer men. But General George Crook knew the enemy was near so he insisted that I take at least five with me in case trouble came our way." The Captain meditated a moment, "As usual it did.

"We were fired upon from ambush by one of the Sioux scouting parties. It was a small one and we soon routed them, but one of my scouts was wounded. Their party scattered and fled back toward their main force. We chased them but decided that since we had so few men we too had better fall back. As we retraced our gallops we found that one of their warriors had been wounded and apparently had lost his horse, as he was on foot. We decided to overtake him if possible as he might give us information if we could catch him. He was easy to trail in the buffalo grass for he was bleeding badly.

"Soon we saw another track also on foot come in contact with the warrior. We dismounted and read the signs. When the two met they had sat down and gone into a powwow. He had been joined by his squaw. Now there were two tracks instead of one. Also they had changed directions.

"Presently we saw why they had changed directions. The

wind began to blow crisply and we saw we were in for a norther. It could drop to several degrees below zero quickly. So we decided to find shelter.

"We scouts rode to a small stream which had a growth of cottonwoods and pitched camp. While three of my scouts gathered plenty of firewood to last us through the night, I doctored my wounded scout; a shot had just grazed his arm.

"The norther died out by sunup and left a clear cold. So we were able to take up the trail where we had left off. It wasn't long until we came to the end of their trail.

"As we approached we saw them lying in the grass as they had huddled together the night before. They had frozen to death.

"His squaw had removed her robe and wrapped it around her wounded mate to keep him from freezing. Then she had placed her body as close to his as possible to help warm his dying body." The Captain paused evidently choking up, then he went on, "We five tough and rough men removed our hats as we stood there in the presence of such devotion."[25]

The footlight fever hit his close friend, Buffalo Bill. Cody wanted Berg to join him. "I told him, Bill, it's coming to a showdown with the Indians. I don't see how you can pull out."

Buffalo Bill laughed, "Why, they won't miss me. They'll think I am still out here, because you and I, even, would get each other mixed if we didn't know the difference."

Buffalo Bill, joined by Texas Jack, made his theatrical bow in New York.[26]

(25) Episode often told by Captain von Berg which is substantiated by Sioux Stories appearing in the Sunday Edition of Southwest-Times Record, Fort Smith, Ark., Nov. 4, 1956.

(26) Lives and Legends of Buffalo Bill—Don Russell.

In Captain von Berg's collection of his paintings was one of Willie Cody when he was just a boy driving the stage in Kansas. (Colonel Cody no doubt was looking over his shoulder at the time, supplying the details.)[27]

Capt. von Berg felt lost without the companionship of Buffalo Bill for when one wasn't staging a prank, they both were. "I sure miss the old coot," Charlie Berg started his discourse, "that brings to my mind," and he chuckled, "the feud between Frank and Luther North and their Pawnee Scouts, and Buffalo Bill. I have worked with Frank and Luther as well as observed them with their Pawnee Scouts in action and they were superb.

"Luther referred to Buffalo Bill as 'showman and buffalo hunter'.[28] On several occasions when their scouting was commendable, Buffalo Bill was given all the credit. Luther North would buck and rear and claim that Buffalo Bill wasn't even there in that particular strategic sector.

"I tried and did somewhat smooth him down. Luther, I said what difference does it make, we are getting our money.

" 'Yes,' he would flare up, 'and doing all the work.'

"That's what I mean, we know that we are doing our duty. That's what we get for having a celebrity as our associate.

"I can't put down what he said to this.

"Now in my case, they don't know I am here. It's Buffalo Bill this and Buffalo Bill that because we look like twins. The only way they can tell us apart is by our horses.

"That brings up another companion scout, Captain Hicks, a Crow Indian. He took such good care of my horse. He joined up with Buffalo Bill's Wild West Show later.

"I don't even know what his Indian name was. I gave

---

(27)   Echoes from the Mountains to the Plains—1907.
(28)   Lives and Legends of Buffalo Bill—Don Russell.

him the name of Captain Hicks and it stuck. He liked it too for he would reiterate, 'Now there's Colonel Cody, Major Frank and Captain Luther and you Captain von Berg and let'd don't leave out Captain Hicks.'

"Captain Hicks was a scout's helper and a good one and I took him along with me every time he was available on many a dangerous mission, especially when we were to be gone several days.

"Washington Irving[29] backs me up in his writings when he said, 'Nothing is more melancholy than the midnight howl of a wolf on a prairie,' and the disturbing part was you didn't know whether it was a sure 'nuff wolf or a sure 'nuff Indian but good old Captain Hicks had a way of telling the difference.

"We would be bedded down, no campfire, our horses tied to us and when the wolves would start their howls, Captain Hicks would answer with some queer sound. I can't even imitate it. The wolves would keep howling and sounding a little closer as Captain Hicks gave out with his weird sound. Presently we would see the outline of a wolf stealthily approaching. Then Captain Hicks would sing out, 'We sleep tonight.' But if no wolves appeared Captain Hicks would whisper, 'Let's get moving, them wolves are Indians.' And we would do just that steal away and forget about sleeping."

"You and I have followed the trail, fought the fight, and returned to camp with many a buck Indian's four top dangling at our belts," so wrote G. T. Propper of Minneapolis to Captain von Berg, March 17, 1917.[30]

"Jack Crawford—he was our poet scout, the only thing soft about him were his words—liked to tell this yarn on me. Said he was going to set it in verse when he got time. If he did I never got to see it. We were up in the Bad Lands. We're being attacked by the Sioux and were ordered to hold

---

(29) A Tour of the Prairies—Washington Irving.

(30) Letter in the University of Arkansas Museum—von Berg Collection.

our fire until we could see the horses' eyes. Charging they came, on their superb war ponies, the Sioux hanging on the offside of their mounts by one leg and one hip and their heads and guns under the horses' necks, their war bonnets trailing like a kite's tail.

"I said out loud, I guess to hear myself think," and Captain von Berg winked, "Yah! I would like to paint that picture.

"Jack Crawford who was beside me, yelled out, 'Let's paint 'em with lead, Charlie Berg'."

When Captain von Berg wasn't scouting or "painting the Indians with lead," he devoted his time to painting the wild life in the West; and although they weren't Audubons, his paintings of a herd of antelope, pair of Rocky Mountain sheep, buffalo bull, blacktail deer, or prairie chickens[31] were carefully and accurately detailed.

When he was in the Indith Basin just east of the Yellowstone River, Montana, he painted a large canvas of "a herd of buffalo traveling south."[32]

One old timer said, "Now, if you get lost, remember that the railroads run east and west and buffalo trails run north and south."[33]

General George Crook and Captain von Berg were hunting and fishing companions for they had much in common. The General was a good shot; he was a naturalist and an expert at trailcraft.[34] General Crook did his own taxidermy[35] and von Berg was an expert at it too.

---

(31)   Echoes from the Mountains to the Plains—1907.

(32)   Same as above.

(33)   Buffalo Land—W. E. Webb (1872).

(34)   On the Border with Crook—John Gregory Bourke.

(35)   Same as above.

Among Captain von Berg's hunting trophies were:[36]

A large buffalo bull's head

Deer heads of blacktail, cottontail and antelope

Horns from buffalo, deer, spike buck, mountain sheep, goat and buck

Tanned skins: buffalo, mountain lion, puma, mountain sheep, grizzly bear, Rocky Mountain antelope and deer

Snake skins of different kinds. (On his old slouch Stetson the band was a snake skin)

A necklace of all kinds of game tusks, teeth and claws.

In 1875, General George Crook was transferred to the Command of the Platte which command was from the Missouri River to the western shore of the Great Salt Lake. Von Berg was a confidential scout of General Crook.

A gendarme with von Berg was Frank Grouard, a famous scout and especially valuable against the Sioux, for when a boy he was captured by the Sioux and lived among them for about six years. Even though he was of French descent, he was a silent man. Frank was a great admirer of Chief Crazy Horse and repeatedly warned General Crook of his masterful tactics in battle.

Someone dubbed Crazy Horse as the Robert E. Lee of the Sioux.[37]

It was rumored about that Frank Grouard wasn't loyal to the troops because of his Sioux upbringing.[38]

---

(36)   Echoes from the Mountains to the Plains—1907—Captain von Berg Collection.

(37)   Death on the Prairie—Paul I. Wellman.

(38)   It was reported that when Frank Grouard was abducted by the Sioux that his home was in Crazy Horse's teepee. This warm feeling for each other was evidenced when Crazy Horse brought his followers into the Red Cloud Agency, April 1877, Crazy Horse was sullen and indifferent except to Frank Grouard.

Von Berg had this to say about Frank Grouard, "You know, we scouts hang together, sort of a tribe all our own, but Frank Grouard was an 'Eagle Scout.' We had our problem that our advice or warnings were not always followed by the 'top brass.' The disastrous example was that of General Custer at Little Big Horn. His scouts told him that the Indians were beyond numbering like the leaves on the cottonwood trees."

(A retired army surgeon wrote years later to Captain von Berg, "I remember you now. You are the scout that followed old Crazy Horse so long, up the Powder River and the Rosebud.")[39]

"I was in sagebrush country, scouting by myself," Captain von Berg related. "Nothing moving except the sagebrush swaying in the wind. Still I had the feeling I was being stalked. I suppose I just acquired this sense from many years of outdoor life. I crouched in the sagebrush and listened and watched for a long time. Still no movement to show where the Indian was. There was a large rock some distance away and I made for it and in going around it, I discovered signs where the Indian had crouched down. That was all I needed for a trail and I followed it. Still I couldn't get sight of the Indian. Soon directly ahead I noticed a patch of sagebrush moving more than that surrounding it, and discovered that the Indian had broken off some sagebrush and tied this on his back as he wiggled snakelike along the ground. Got 'Old Betsy' in action. See that scalp over there with a bit of sagebrush in the hair?"[40]

Indian scouts were not only guides, scouts and interpreters but intermediaries between the Generals and Indian Chiefs.

------

(39) Letter in the University of Arkansas Museum—Captain von Berg Collection

(40) This experience recalled by Ward Mayes, Meridian, Idaho—tape recording—nephew of Mrs. Martha Louisa von Berg, Captain von Berg's second wife.

Captain von Berg had such a duty. "General Crook called me in his tent one day and gave me a mission I shall remember long. I was to go to Sitting Bull and Crazy Horse to counsel with them regarding negotiations just before the all-out Sioux War.

"It was an effort on the part of the General to avoid a showdown with the Sioux. I was to go with presents which he furnished, and confer with the Sioux leaders. He said, as the Indians knew me so well that he hoped their leaders would listen to me. The Sioux considered me their friend as I had traded with them a number of years back. So I went alone riding my own mount and leading a pack horse with the presents for the chiefs and their squaws.

"When I got into Sioux territory I met a scouting group and waited for them to carry the news to their camp that I was on my way to see Sitting Bull and Crazy Horse.

"In a short time I had instructions to proceed to the teepee of Crazy Horse. A group of Sioux warriors escorted me to the edge of the camp, from where other warriors took me to the teepee of Crazy Horse. It was sometime in the afternoon when I arrived. The old warrior met me very courteously. I sat cross-legged as he sat, while he lighted the pipe of peace, puffed on it and passed it to me. That part of the ceremony over, he asked my mission, saying his warriors had told him that I carried a message from the Big General and the Little White Father in Washington. I assured him that was so. Then he asked me if I had eaten my midday meal. When I told him I had not had time to eat, he said he would call his squaw and have something brought.

"His number one squaw soon appeared bringing my meal and a pitcher of water. Remember this, that so far as I know, no Indian learned to make an alcoholic drink. That was one of the curses the white man was to pass to the Indians from his civilization.

"I was hungry, and the maize loaf—corn pone the white man called it—and the meat were good. I ate with relish. The Chief said nothing until I had pushed the little basket aside.

"Then he smiled and asked me if I knew what the meat was. I told him I thought it fish.

"He chuckled as only Crazy Horse could chuckle and said, 'You have been eating rattlesnake, my white friend.'

"It was such a delicacy that I asked Crazy Horse how they prepared it.

" 'We only have to be careful that the snake does not bite himself, then prepare and cook as a fish,' he told me.

"Crazy Horse listened very attentively to my message and plea as a friend.

"Then he told me very emphatically that he could not accept the proposition from my General. He felt too much would be sacrificed by his Nation. He expressed his regret that we could not be one at the council fire.

"He gave me an escort of warriors to the edge of the Sioux Territory. There they waved friendly good-byes as they wheeled their ponies to head for their camp. Sadly I realized that the next time we met we would meet as enemies.

"As I turned toward my own camp, my horses disturbed a rattlesnake for he rattled his warning. I wanted to stop and catch him for supper but I had too urgent a message to relay to General Crook."[41]

Captain von Berg's Winchester (engraved on name plate,

(41) Episode often told by Captain von Berg which is substantiated by Sioux Stories appearing in the Sunday Edition of Southwest-Times Record, Fort Smith, Ark., Nov. 11, 1956.

"Old Betsy," Chas. L. V. Berg) was his truest friend for 30 years.[42]

"I'll never forget the model No. 1876. The number made no impression on me until the year, 1876. We called it the 'Bloody '76.'

"I'll go along with what an old timer said, 'We would be fighting the Indians yet if the buffaloes had not been killed off.'[43]

"This was the year for the pincers movement of the U. S. troops. The strategy was to converge on the Sioux from both flanks simultaneous; quite similar to the plan General P. R. Connor, Colonel Walker and Colonel Cole had attempted back in 1865, which resulted in the Indians being more impressed with their own prowess.[44]

"General Alfred Terry in command, General George Crook, General John Gibbon, and reduced from rank, General Custer were all in the field.

"The year's major engagements started early, March 17, Colonel Reynolds versus Chief Crazy Horse in which Colonel Reynolds pulled out so fast that he left his wounded to fall into the hands of the Sioux.

"Then Chief Crazy Horse menaced General Crook, asking for a fight and he got it on June 17 at Rosebud. Some historians give General Crook a victory at Rosebud and a few marked it up as a defeat."

Captain von Berg expressed himself dogmatically about the Battle of the Rosebud, "You will not find the Battle of the Rosebud given much space in your history books but it was one of the hardest fought American troops have ever taken part in. I looked the other day in a history book and

---

(42) Gun in University of Arkansas Museum—Captain von Berg Collection.

(43) Death on the Prairie—Paul I. Wellman.

(44) Powder River—Struthers Burt.

could not find the battle at all. I am here to tell you though the Sioux were superb horsemen and good fighters in their own way. We were beaten fairly and beaten badly at Rosebud.[45]

"Remember, I told you I would tell you how Crazy Horse nearly out-generaled George Crook at Rosebud. Yah! General Crook's army was too big to tackle as one unit, so Chief Crazy Horse reckoned that if he could divide General Crook's forces, he could wipe out each segment in turn.

"General Crook sent Captain Anson Mills along the Rosebud in pursuit of a feint retreat by the Sioux. Chief Crazy Horse's strategy was working perfectly. Who called the General's attention—in pretty rough language—to his mistake, I'm not saying. Then General Crook recalled Captain Mills and his forces got back in the nick of time."[46]

The aftermath of the Battle of the Rosebud brings up this story of Captain von Berg.

Whether duels between the top echelon and Indian chiefs were conceptions of Ned Buntline for his dime-novels —the best sellers in those days—or the showmanship of Buffalo Bill (the Billy Rose of his day) nevertheless they were "fab".

General Custer (Yellow Hair) was supposed to have fought a duel with an Indian Chief, son of Sitting Bull (which was the cause of the strong enmity of Sitting Bull for General Custer). However this was not substantiated.

Buffalo Bill was likewise credited with a duel against Yellow Hand but this was not authenticated either.[47]

So, the duel of Captain von Berg which was not recorded

---

(45)   Paragraph at bottom of first column, Sioux Stories, Southwest-Times Record, Oct. 21, 1956.

(46)   This battle maneuver verified by: Death on the Prairie—Paul I. Wellman; Warpath and Bivouac—Finerty; With Crook at the Rosebud—Vaughn.

(47)   The Lives and Legends of Buffalo Bill—Don Russell.

in the annals of General Crook could be of the same cloth. Chief Yellow Dog who was the Sioux challenger is not listed among the archives[48] but the difficulty in translation of an Indian name should be taken into consideration.

This is the way von Berg told it, "It was soon after the Battle of the Rosebud. I had a group of 10 scouts under my charge with orders to report directly to General George Crook, all moves made by the Sioux. The Sioux were feeling their strength. We were in a poor state of morale. That was when I received a challenge to fight a duel.

"Chief Yellow Dog, a young Sioux chieftain sent a challenge to 'Eagletail,' chief of the army scouts to fight a duel with him to show whether he was all that a scout should be and all the Sioux believed him to be. He, Chief Yellow Dog, did not believe that the 'Eagletail' one, was all that he was thought to be. I went to General Crook with the challenge. The general did not want me to fight the duel as he was afraid something might happen and he said he did not want to lose my services. He was not quite sure of me, but I was not afraid for I knew the chief, who had sent the challenge personally. I assured him everything would go all right with me. There was some planning to do.

"I sent the reply back to Yellow Dog that I thought the duel could be arranged. But I wanted Chief Crazy Horse to handle the arrangements for him. I would have General Crook handle my part of the challenge. A reply came back that Chief Crazy Horse was the one he had selected to handle his.

"Three days later, according to arrangement, General Crook met Chief Crazy Horse 10 miles from the fort, so that no surprises were possible either way, as each had just so many warriors with him. Plans were completed. Neither Yellow Dog nor I were present.

"Plans laid down for the duel said that we were to meet

---

(48) Letter dated July 19, 1965 from Smithsonian Institution, Washington, D. C.

at a given point so many miles from the fort. Each contestant was to have two weapons only. Both contestants were to be mounted. Each group, army and Indians were to form a line east and west so that the sun would be equally strong for both contestants as they would be facing north and south. The army was to face the north or take up a position on the south while the Sioux were to face south or take up their position on the north. That placed each with their camp behind them. The contest ground was well selected for it was perfectly level. A line was to be formed by each force 350 yards apart so that horses would have room to maneuver, yet be seen by both sides. The show was well set up.

"The morning came for the duel and the general asked me how I was feeling and if he should call it off, as he did not believe in duels even under that kind of condition. I told him to let it go through as the army's reputation would be ruined now if we stopped it. So his contingent got ready. As we rode on the set for the duel the Indians rode on from the other direction.

"General Crook met Crazy Horse with five men each, halfway between the lines. Yellow Dog chose a tomahawk and a knife as his weapons. When I learned what he had chosen, I chose a knife, this one," and Captain von Berg handled a certain knife in his collection fondly, "and 'Old Betsy.'

"The army was to fire a signal shot when ready. The Indians were to fire an answering shot if they too were ready. All was to wait that second shot then the contestants were to ride toward each other and the dual would be kicked off.

"I thought, I knew the Sioux well enough to know what Yellow Dog had in mind for that tomahawk. They were good with them and Yellow Dog was one of the best for all Sioux tried to reach his standards with this weapon.

"The morning was perfect with a warm sun at our backs and just enough chill in the air to give us pep. I had chosen my own black stallion and Yellow Dog was mounted on a wiry spotted stallion he owned.

"I shall never forget that array of painted savages on their line. Neither will I ever forget the stern faced cavalrymen behind me as I took my position. Then with me on line our shot was fired and theirs answered immediately. Both horses jumped forward.

"Yellow Dog grasped his tomahawk in his right hand. So he was putting great faith in that hatchet of his. We rode straight at each other, neither one veering the least and each horse in a dead run.

"As we approached, Yellow Dog raised on his pony and came down with a smashing blow aimed at my skull.

"I raised 'Old Betsy' and took the blow on the barrel.

"Both of us wheeled our mounts immediately and were facing each other at about the same instant. I raised 'Old Betsy' and fired. Yellow Dog was rolling on the ground. I had aimed at his right shoulder and the shot was true as his shoulder was shattered and the tomahawk was gone. He got off the ground and signalled his horse away. The horse trotted away a few yards and started grazing.

"I was now at great advantage as my opponent was dismounted and had only a knife. To show the Indians that I was not afraid of their challenger I dismounted and signalled my horse away. I then placed my right hand behind me and drew my knife with my left hand. Yellow Dog had already drawn his knife, having to clutch it in his left hand.

"You have heard the fans 'whoop it up' when their team makes a good play on the football field. Well, that is exactly what the Sioux did. They gave a great big yell for me as I gave their warrior a break which the rules did not allow him.

"We rushed at each other like two wildcats, our knife-blades shining in the sun.

"No," and the "Old Scout" reflected, "I didn't scalp him. He put up such a brave fight." [49]

June 25, 1876 marks the date of the tragic Custer Massacre at Little Big Horn.

Captain von Berg relates, "The day of the massacre, I was enroute from General Terry to General Custer carrying a dispatch. Toward evening I noticed a lone Indian riding toward me. So I was ready for him. When he got closer he hailed me and I recognized him. He was one of the Crow scouts. 'Curley' some of us called him (his Indian name was Cola Wamba) was attached to General Custer. Sadly he told me what had happened. Then when he saw that every man would be killed he grabbed up a Sioux blanket from a dead Sioux and disguised himself that way and made his way out of the carnage. Knowing Indians, I didn't ask 'Curley' to go back with me. But I increased my caution the rest of the way.

"I picked up two other scouts and we made our way to the scene of the battle. We looked over the battlefield trying to find the body of General Custer. I knew Crazy Horse was a great admirer of the general and I knew the respect which the Sioux held for 'Yellow Hair.' Yah! He was bareheaded. One side of the hair was matted with blood from a wound but his scalp was untouched. That was a high tribute of the Sioux's respect for a worthy enemy." The Captain bowed his head as he concluded, "All the other men had been scalped." [50]

Quoting Major William A. Bell in his *Echoes from the Mountains to the Plains*, "Captain Berg remembers well the famous charge of Custer, as he was stationed only a few miles from the scene where it happened. While he would

---

(49)   Episode often told by Captain von Berg which is substantiated by Sioux Stories appearing in the Sunday Edition of Southwest-Times Record, Fort Smith, Ark., Oct. 21, 1956.

(50)   Feature story, Arkansas Gazette, Little Rock, Nov. 1, 1964.

not detract from Custer's glory, he thinks it was a needless sacrifice brought about by foolhardiness. Captain Berg describes in a very realistic manner the way in which Custer allowed himself to be surrounded by the Sioux, the Cheyennes and the Arapahoes, and says that this awful massacre could have been prevented by a little precaution on Custer's part."

In the von Berg collection is a portrait of General Custer.[51]

A significant discovery was made in the collection of paintings by Charles von Berg in the archives of the University of Arkansas Museum. It is a portrait of an Indian. The details of the face are quite expressive. He is clad in breach cloth and moccasins with tops (like mukluks) holding his gun, wearing ammunition belt with revolver in holster, necklace and bracelet. In the distant background are snow clad mountains and lots of sky. In the foreground are a conifer forest and, to each side, a large boulder.

No identification whatsoever on the painting.

The discovery—and quite appropriately so—was made by the Historical Society of Montana, Miss Mary K. Dempsey. The writer had sent them a picture of this painting as it looked quite Montanaish, to see if they could identify the Indian.

Miss Dempsey sent back a copease copy of their photograph of "Curley," the lone survivor of Custer's Last Stand, and said that they could see "quite a close resemblance" between the two.

A second examination of this portrait revealed no more than the first, until it was put under a special light which revealed in the lower right-hand corner under the buffalo grass in Captain von Berg's printing:

---

(51) Echoes from the Mountains to the Plains—1907—Captain von Berg Collection.

Curley
Lone Survivor of Custer's Massacre
June 25, 1876

Doubtless this is the only portrait of "Curley", the Crow Scout with Custer.[52]

The Indian scouts lost their Charley Reynolds at Little Big Horn. He was with Major Reno's detachment.

Ironically, it was Charley Reynolds who brought the news of the gold strike in the Black Hills when he was with Custer on his Missouri Expedition back in 1874.[53]

Captain von Berg cleared up one point, "In such a battle as the Little Big Horn many things escaped being put into the records. Just as your history book says Sitting Bull was the commander of the Sioux. Yet, I know that Sitting Bull never left his teepee during the battle and that Crazy Horse was the commander of the field. These things happened due partly to our misunderstanding of Indian organization."[54]

Paradoxically, the American Eagle screamed all over the land about the Custer's Massacre. The military was savagely criticized. Congressional investigation acted as a balm of Gilead. A small minority group—most of them had not been West, yet they knew all the answers—took the Indians' side, that of being ejected from their rightful land.

President Grant kept his usual complacency for he knew that his generals in the field were slowly tightening the cordon about the Indians. Inwardly he must have chuckled

(52) Courtesy of Dr. Chas. R. McGimsey, Curator University of Arkansas Museum. This portrait has been on loan basis to Amon Carter Museum, Fort Worth.

(53) Famous Frontiersmen—E. G. Cattermole, Courtesy of University of Oklahoma Library.

(54) Substantiated by Sioux Stories, 1st column Southwest-Times Record, Fort Smith, Ark., Oct. 28, 1956.

over the thought, "That's just what I got throughout the War Between the States."

General Miles came up the Powder River country, General Crook and General Gibbon flanking him.

Nov. 1876, General Ranald Mackenzie wiped out Dull Knife's forces.

Chief Crazy Horse took on General Miles but Crazy Horse's scouts couldn't see under the tarpaulins of the covered wagons. Instead of being used for hauling soldiers they had wagon guns in them.

April, 1877, Chief Crazy Horse led his followers to the Red Cloud Agency. In the fall of that year Chief Crazy Horse was killed at the reservation.

Sitting Bull took his people across the border into Canada.

October 1878, a powwow was held at Fort Walsh, Canada between General Terry and Sitting Bull.

At the beginning of that year 1879, Dull Knife and Little Wolf led their Cheyenne followers from the agency to return to their lands in Montana. The winter was at its worst. Dull Knife's group was killed out but Little Wolf made what was an impossible trek—with the army endeavoring to locate them on the way and turn them back—and reached Montana. And it had a happy ending, this brave band was permitted to stay.

The West was a far cry from being safe for the swarm of settlers and miners going up into the Powder River country and the grass range. As late as 1880, Fort Maginnis was built. Close by sprang up a mining town, Giltedge, which later went the way of other ghost towns.[55]

Captain von Berg tells about his experience in this region. "I had been detailed as scout to carry a troop of

_____

(55) University of Montana, quoted in Montana Almanac 1956-60, page 326, "Dismantled by civilians later".

soldiers from Fort Livingston to Fort Maginnis. When on the way the Major—I'm not sure of his name although I think it was Bell—who had charge of the soldiers suggested that I take three or four troopers and kill several antelopes as we were in need of some fresh meat.

"We were nearly 100 miles from any settlement but I directed Major Bell to follow a trail until a point 20 miles away and to wait for me there. I then entered the woods with my four troopers. I soon became separated from my companions and had proceeded some distance when I saw deer. I dismounted and as was my custom left my mount untied to graze. I concealed myself and waited. When the deer came within range of 'Old Betsy' I easily killed two, and running down to where my game lay, I heard a terrific noise behind me. At first I thought that it was a herd of buffalo that had been disturbed by my shooting but I soon perceived with horror that it was a drove of about 200 wild horses and that they had already cut me off from my horse. Wild horses always surround any domestic animal that may be in their way and carry it off with the drove. This they did with my mount. I followed the horses as best I could, trying to whistle back my mount. But bad luck never comes alone for upon hearing a second noise even more terrifying than the first, I saw that I was directly in the path of probably 100 mad, charging steers. There was a rocky eminence in front of me. I made a desperate effort to reach it, clinging to 'Old Betsy' although twice I tripped over her and fell headlong. I stumbled up the rocks, cutting my face and hands but at last gained the top. All around me the steers gathered in fury. Heads down, feet pawing or rearing up in determined effort to reach me. I clung to the rocks until I had regained my breath, then picking out steers on the far edge I fired eight times. Immediately the animals turned and charged the eight carcasses. I stayed on the rocks all night. Early dawn when I woke, the steers were gone and my faithful mount was standing by the rocks."

When questioned further the Old Scout replied, "Yes, I found my four troopers and we killed more deer. Were the Major and the boys glad to see us or the fresh meat?" as he chuckled, "I don't know which."[56]

1880, Ann, Captain von Berg's only daughter was born.

Charles von Berg returned home and set up his guide and hunting service. He had some cards "struck off" which read:

Chas. L. V. Berg
Practical
Guide and Hunter
to the Rockies
Box 997
Le Mars, Iowa.

Von Berg, like the buffaloes, roamed over the West. He was in Texas, Colorado, Wyoming, Montana and California.

Sitting Bull brought his followers back into the United States and surrendered to General Miles at Fort Keogh, Montana.

When General Crook was sent back to the Southwest in 1882 to round up the Apaches and Geronimo in particular, von Berg was with him.

There he found time to paint for he forwarded to some of his friends, instead of post cards, small paintings on leaves of the century plant—which is common in desert areas in the Southwest and Mexico.[57] One of these showing a greyhound chasing a jackrabbit is in the University of Oklahoma Museum, Norman, Oklahoma.

Captain von Berg brought back a photograph made by a Denver photographer of the Aztec ruins in New Mexico. This picture shows the magnitude of these ruins with the

---

(56) Echoes from the Mountains to the Plains, 1907—Major Wm. A. Bell and Sunday Magazine—St. Louis Post-Pispatch—October 7, 1917.

(57) Dr. Patricia Rand, University of Arkansas—Botany Department.

Knickerbocker Mountains in the background and the profusion of the "chico" brush in the foreground.

Captain von Berg posed in this picture but was all but camouflaged by the ruin and "chico" brush.[58]

In the von Berg collection is a miniature loom, a facsimile of those used by the Navahoes. It shows the Navaho pattern about half completed of tight knit blanketlike material.[59]

Scout von Berg did not stay the year out in the Southwest. On Nov. 14, 1882 he killed a large buffalo bull on the Yellowstone River in Montana, which he mounted and it is the one in his collection. The Old Scout said that the Smithsonian Institution offered him $500 for this trophy.[60]

A pass on the Northern Pacific Railroad Company to Captain von Berg dated Sept. 22, 1884, read: "You will pass baggage, including guns, dogs and hunting outfit for party of four (4) free anywhere on this line."[61]

In this interim Charlie von Berg met Theodore Roosevelt who had a ranch in the Dakota Territory—15 miles north of Medora.[62]

Chas. L. von Berg's Rockies were gradually being fenced

----

(58) The description of this Pueblo ruin was graciously furnished by C. J. Thomasson, Special Collection Dept. Zimmerman Library, the University of New Mexico.

(59) University of Arkansas Museum—Captain von Berg Collection.

(60) Sunday Magazine—St. Louis Post-Dispatch—October 7, 1917. S. C. Dellinger, Curator of the University of Arkansas Museum at the time the von Berg Collection was catalogued, said of this buffalo head that the history connected with this was, when this buffalo was skinned a number of arrowheads were found in the mane and in the folds of tough skin on the neck.

(61) Letter in the University of Arkansas Museum—Captain von Berg Collection.

(62) When Vice-President Teddy Roosevelt became President the von Berg family remembers the Old Scout saying "I knew him when he was a rancher in the Dakota Territory."

in not only with barbed wire but with states' restrictions as to hunting.

In 1886 he received the following letter in answer to his:

Fort Meade, D. T.
August 30th. 1886

Dear Sir:

In regard to finding Elk the Big Horn Mountains is the nearest locality—the Crow Indians hunt them however on the heads of the Tongue, Little Horn & Powder. Last year the garrison at Fort McKinney got 6 six mule team loads of elk deer & antelope near Old Fort Casper south of here they are to be found also in the Bighorn Basin where I got sheep also in 1884—also a couple of old buffalo bulls. The best antelope & deer shooting I imagine in the U. S. is on the heads of the Belle Fourche & Cheyenne Rivers in Wyoming near Pumpkin buttes as soon as the weather gets cold they are in there by the thousand & winter there.

Wyoming has passed a law forbidding non-residents to hunt at all in the Territory or resident to kill more than one deer antelope etc a day & that even during certain seasons— or to transport game from the limit of the Ty. penalty for each offence $100.

The Cattle Association in Cheyenne is connected with the game protection clubs in some way so that a great many cattlemen on the range protect the game & enforce the laws against strangers. There is some deer hunting on the lower Powder Little Missouri in Montana & the only other place I know of any is on the Sioux reservation where I would not advise any one to try for it. I would try the Big Horn the country I first mentioned if I wanted to fit out a party & could go where I wanted to.

In '82 some men were hunting on the Sioux reservation on the Upper Grand River and were said to have 1500 deer skins—they were captured by the Indian police taken over to the Missouri at Yates thence to Bismarck & were up before the U. S. Court but what became of them finally I never heard but they lost one 4 horse team their deer and buffalo hides, wagon, blankets, rifles etc.

The Indians never bother the Military and as I talk their language & know a great many of them personally I hunt there whenever I feel like it and am never molested but I hear that my favorite hunting grounds have been burnt over this year. There is no hunting about this part of the country worth mentioning as it is fenced in and farmed, there are a few white tail within a radius of 6 or 8 miles of the Post in the heavy pine timber but it is of no use to hunt them without long eared hounds & there is but one that I know of in the Black Hills, there are several bear also in the same section that come within a mile of here at night. I go off from 60 to 100 miles & stay from 20 to 30 days—camping out—but I am going to miss my hunt this year & next to my sorrow.

Thanking you again for your kindness about the dogs, I am truly yours

H. L. Scott
Lieut. 7th Cav'y [63]

Lieut. Scott was one of the few soldiers who learned to know the Indians. He studied the way their minds worked and was therefore one of the few soldiers ever trusted by the Indians. [64]

Lieut. Scott advanced to the rank of General. When Buffalo Bill died January 10, 1917, General Scott was among the first to wire condolence to the family. [65]

Evidently from Captain von Berg's inquiry to Lieut.

------

(63) Letter in the University of Arkansas Museum—Captain von Berg Collection.

(64) Powder River—Struthers Burt.

(65) The Lives and Legends of Buffalo Bill—Don Russell.

Scott, he surmised that his guide and hunting service was on its way out.

Charlie Berg felt more at home in his West than he did at Le Mars. His family had practically grown up without him so at best he was more like a relative than husband and father.

He resided in the West, hunting and fishing with his old friends.

At the T E, Buffalo Bill's famous ranch located in the heart of the Rocky Mountains von Berg met his old friend, Wm. A. Bell who also was a family friend of the Codys.

These three Iowa boys were a close entente, due no doubt to their close resemblance to each other.[66]

This Wm. A. Bell is not the Wm. A. Bell of the Denver and Rio Grande Western Railroad Company fame. In fact, there is no relation.[67]

Von Berg and Buffalo Bill (both pranksters as we already know) conferred on Wm. A. Bell the rank of Major, and from then on he was Major Bell to his friends.

Major Bell was from Sigourney, Iowa and was a printer.

He came West to strike it rich and did.

Major Bell named his only son, Cody Bell, after Colonel Cody.[68]

Cody Bell wore his hair long like his namesake until he was grown and enlisted for World War I.[69]

---

(66) Wm. A. Bell's daughter, Mrs. May Bell Harris, San Francisco writes, "looking so much like 'Buffalo Bill' as he had been taken many times for him by photographers and in papers."

(67) Mrs. May Bell Harris, sister of Cody Bell writes, "Now for the William Abraham Bell—he is of no kin—know nothing of him."

(68) Echoes from the Mountains to the Plains, 1907—Wm. A. Bell.

(69) Mrs. Joe Flanagan (Ruth Mayes) niece of Captain von Berg's second wife remembers Cody Bell when he and his father visited Captain von Berg and verifies his long hair and added, "Buffalo Bill asked him not to cut his hair and he didn't until he joined the army in World War I."

Quoting from *Echoes from the Mountains to the Plains* by Major Wm. A. Bell published in 1907:

"Col. W. F. Cody, 'Buffalo Bill' and his young friend and protege, Leonard Cody Bell. The Colonel is very fond of his young friend and they have had many a romp together on the Colonel's T E Ranch in Wyoming. Leonard is also a bosom friend of Capt. Von Berg's having visited the latter recently."

At the T E Ranch Captain von Berg painted many scenes around the ranch.

Too, von Berg painted a large copy of the famous painting of Colonel Cody on his favorite saddler, "Tucker", by the renowned artist, Rosa Bonheur.[70]

It was on one of his visits to the T E ranch that he did his painting of the Shoshone River. It was one of his best: one could feel the placidity of the river and the country.

Now don't laugh at that statement for this is somewhat of a parallel. This was fairly recent, Mr. Thomas Gilcrease was looking at a Frederic Remington painting of "Going on the Warpath"—done in sepia tones—which belongs to Jack Holt, Fayetteville, Ark. As they looked at the painting, Mr. Gilcrease said, "Be quiet, Jack." Jack listened for a second or two and then spoke out, "I don't hear anything." Mr. Gilcrease whispered, "Sh-h! Can't you hear the hoofbeats of those Indian ponies?"

Without adieu, von Berg disappeared from the West which was true to his philosophy, "Scouts don't say goodbye."

---

(70) Echoes from the Mountains to the Plains, 1907—Captain von Berg Collection.

VI

"Scouts Don't Say Goodbye..."

Back in the early 1900s, Mrs. Julia Cody Goodman, sister of Buffalo Bill (Col. William F. Cody) addressed a letter:

> Capt. Charles L. von Berg
> Ledge of East Mountain
> Fayetteville, Ark.[1]

"Nein," and the Old Scout would shake his head slowly to attractive offers from the silent movies and the chatauquas,

(1) Letter in von Berg Collection—University of Arkansas Museum.

CODY BELL

MAJOR WM. A. BELL   "OLD SCOUT"

CHRISTMAS WITH BUFFALO BILL, 1905, AT HIS TE RANCH

and the standing offer from his friend, Colonel Cody to join his show. "I couldn't make a spectacle of what we paid for with blood and heartaches."

His spirit typifying the heart of the West is exemplified in the following poem:

'Twas Christmas of the border
　　When the West was wild and young;
Before the days of railroads,
　　When many a horse-thief swung;
When men, to seek their fortunes,
　　Took their lives into their hands,
And dug and washed for gold dust
　　In those far off golden sands.

It was rough, I tell you partner,
　　Out in those mining camps,
With none but rough, big bearded men
　　Whose memory on me stamps
The fact, that 'neath the woolen shirt,
　　There beat big hearts and true,
And tender as a woman's
　　And honest through and through.

The games were not as gentle
　　As tennis and croquet,
'Twas fashion to play poker there
　　And bags of dust the pay.
A mile or so from our gulch,
　　A washerwoman lived,
Whose little children ate and wore
　　From what she scraped and saved.

This Christmas night I tell about,
　　One of the boys was out;
He saw the washerwoman's light,
　　And turned him right about.
Straight for the lighted cabin—
　　For he was looking 'round
For a gang of thieves and outlaws,
　　The cabin's light he found.

With tiger tread he hastened,
  "I've found them in their den"
Thought he "and now I'll listen,
  I think I've got my men."
With hand upon his pistol
  He neared the cabin door,
And listened to the voices
  Then could not wait for more.

And this is what the brave scout heard
  Out on the border wilds:
"Oh, Ma! to-morrow's Christmas!"
  The sweet voice was a child's,
"And will good Santa Claus come down
  And bring us toys and slates
And pretty dolls and candies too,
  Like he used to in the States?"

"God grant he may" the mother sighed
  "But I am not so sure,
That Santa Claus will be so kind—
  Now that we are so poor.
But go to bed my darlings,
  And say your evening prayer;
Remember God is in the West
  As well as way back there."

The scout went to the window
  Through which the bright light shone
He saw her kiss the children,
  "God bless you both, my own!"
"Gol danged if I can stand it;"
  The Scout brushed away a tear
To which his eyes a stranger
  Had been for many a year.

The children went to bed then,
  And left the mother there,
And overcome with bitter grief,
  She knelt in earnest prayer;
"Oh God!" she said and weeping
  "Remove this bitter cup;
How can I bear to cross them,
  They've hung their stockings up.

"I've not a slice of bacon
    Or crust of bread to eat,
When they awake for breakfast,
    Nor nothing good nor sweet;
Thy will be done, oh Father
    But if it be thy will,
Oh, let me get some clothes and wood
    To ward off cold and chill."

'Twas too much for the hardy scout,
    He turned to move away,
But heard the children's voices,
    And to hear what they would say
He neared their bedroom window,
    And while he waited there,
He listened to their lisping,
    As they raised their voice in prayer.

"O Dod bless our dear mama,
    Who works so hard all day;
And buys good things for us to eat,
    When the miners come and pay.
And Dod you know she loves you,
    And don't like folks what swears,
And makes her little children
    Kneel down and say dere prayers.

"And Dod, it taint much trouble,
    I'll ask some more, because
You see to-night is Christmas,
    And please send Santa Claus
To put fings in our stockings,
    We hung dem up out there;
Susie's by the chimney,
    And mine is on the chair.

"Now Dod please don't dis'point us,
    Just send whatever suits,
Send Sis a pair of nice warm shoes
    And me a pair of boots.
And Dod please send a blanket,
    This cover's awful thin,
And big cracks all through the house,
    They let the cold in.

"Now Dod I'll say dood night to you,
    Because I'se awful cold,
And if I ask for too much things
    You'll think I'se getting bold.
But if you please, before you go,
    I'll ask you—this is all—
If it aint too expensive
    Send my poor ma a shawl."

"You bet your life He will my boy,"
    The scout said soft and low—
Then turned away with silent tread,
    Then to the camp did go.
"Wake up fellers, one and all
    And ante up with me,
I'll show you how to gamble
    In a way you'll like to see."

"Now what's excited Buffalo Bill
    I wonder" shouted one;
"Just listen" said the border scout
    "While through my talk I run."
And then he told the story through,
    The facts set plain and clear,
And many a rough old miner's hand
    Arose and brushed a tear.

"Now here's a twenty dollar piece,
    Who'll ante up with me
To make the little children
    Go wild and dance with glee?"
The poker tables bore rich fruit,
    The stacks of gold heaped high,
"I'll go you one and raise you two,"
    "I'll stay with you or die."

Bill took his hat and passed it 'round,
    "Be lively, boys, because
Before the sun is up, you know,
    We'll all be Santa Claus."
The boys chipped in their coin and dust
    Like men who business meant,
And then from out that gambling den
    To another one they went.

And told the story o'er again,
    The same results all round,
And others joined the merry throng
    And "chink" the gold did sound.
They went the rounds of all saloons
    And gambling dens in camp,
With big, rough honest hearts for light
    And torches for a lamp.

It warn't no scrimping crowd you bet,
    The money poured like rain;
The rough old miners stood not back
    Nor were their efforts vain.
The money came, the crowd increased,
    Then they went to the store;
To buy the things the children wished
    Warm clothes, and food and more

Than had been thought or wished for
    By the children while at prayer,
Or the mother in her fondest wish
    For her little darlings there.
And many a miner rough choked up,
    At the thought of cruel fates,
For some had wives and loved ones
    Way back in the States.

They heaped a pile of everything
    The border store contained,
For the widow and her children,
    Until nothing else remained
For them to do, but get it there
    To the widow's lowly home
Then was their night's work finished,
    And they abroad could roam.

There was lots of us rough fellows,
    (For I was in the crowd,)
And each man gathered up a load,
    Though no one spoke aloud.
And then led on by Cody
    To the widow's lonely hut
Across the gulch, beyond the hill,
    We took the shortest cut.

Then quiet every miner bold
   Deposited his load
Before the little cabin door,
   Then gathered in the road;
And in that pile was everything
   The widow could desire;
And of pure virgin gold a sack
   Still made the pile raise higher.

And to the sack they tied a note
   Which bade the widow cheer,
And said: "accept this Christmas gift
   From One whose always near.
For God has heard your children's prayer
   And this is here because
It was your darlings' earnest wish
   And God sent Santa Claus."

"Who'll stand guard till day break?"
   "Buffalo Bill" said Cy,
"And with his trusty rifle
   He'll guard the gift or die."
A man all clad in buckskin
   Stepped out and said "I will!"
The miners knew the gift was safe,
   The man was Buffalo Bill.

On the Christmas morning
   She opened wide the door,
And an avalanche of Christmas
   Came tumbling on the floor.
And the Children heard the rumble
   Of the gift, and without pause
They came in from their bedroom
   And shouted "Santa Claus!"

The widow knelt beside them
   Despite their childish pranks,
With streaming eyes and fuller heart,
   Returned to God her thanks.

*   *   *   *   *   *   *   *

And stealthy through the bushes
   There moved off one so still,
"God bless you little cubs," said he,
   Then vanished Buffalo Bill.

Note from publisher of the above poem, Wm. A. Bell:

"While visiting at the home of Col. Cody, December 25, 1904 at the famous T E ranch, Mrs. Julia Cody Goodman, a sister of Col. Cody read this poem.

"It was one she had stored away with other rememberances of her brother. I thoroughly enjoyed it and brought it with me and I have reproduced it in this form for Mrs. Goodman; the author is unknown to her."[2]

Mrs. Goodman had this to say, "This poem is a true story of a western mining camp in the dreary Black Hills of Wyoming and was written by a friend of Buffalo Bill's in the year 1869, when he was scouting around Ft. Laramie."

In the latter part of 1887, Captain von Berg appeared in Fayetteville, Ark. With his long hair, western hat and buckskin jacket with fringe, Captain von Berg created a bit of excitement for the word got around that Buffalo Bill was in town.

Louis von Berg—his enlisted name—remembered the boys of the 18th, 19th, 20th Iowa Regiments relating about the Ozarks and having a bad case of Wanderlust and a touch of nostalgia for his Black Forest, came to sight that part of Arkansas.

He rode over the hills "a-horseback"; eyed the fishing streams, White River, Kings River and Buffalo River.

He liked what he saw, and as was his trigger action with "Old Betsy", in January 1888, he bought an 80 acre ranch out from Fayetteville near a small town of Goshen.[3]

None of his family would leave the tall corn country of Iowa except his youngest boy, Bill.

------

(2) Mrs. May Bell Harris of San Francisco, daughter of Major Wm. A. Bell in her letter dated Feb. 15, 1965 wrote: "The little poem of Buffalo Bill as Santa Claus was anonymous I remember that—and Mrs. J. C. G. was Buffalo Bill's sister."

(3) Deed dated 2nd day of January, 1888 recorded, page 472, Washington County Deed Records.

Together they bached on the ranch. Father and son got to know each other for the first time. Bill was like his father in that he was bubbling over with devilment and each one tried to outdo the other with pranks.

Charlie Berg hitched his two spotted ponies to his buggy and started to town. Something was wrong with the buggy. Instead of the seat being level it would tilt to the right at a sharp angle and then to the left. Then too he had to keep jerking on one rein to keep the buggy out of the ditch. He hailed a neighbor he was passing on the road who started laughing and when he could stop told Charlie to look at his wheels. Berg looked at his front wheels and then at the back wheels. He discovered that one front wheel and the diagonal back wheel had been interchanged. "Yah!" he laughed. "I'll get even with Bill." [4]

The von Bergs had a sow which preferred the garden to the hog lot and she would lift up the fence with her snout and help herself. To teach the old sow a lesson Charlie Berg peppered her with a light bird shot load which put her on the run and out of the garden. Bill was present at the time. Watching his chance he changed the load in the shotgun to a heavy load. The next time the sow couldn't resist getting into the garden, Bill's father let her have it. As soon as the shot went off, Captain von Berg knew what had happened by the percussion of the gun, but it was too late, the sow was dead. [5]

All the while—although Captain von Berg was the only one that knew it—he was looking for a second wife.

When he found the one of his choice, Captain von Berg waged a fast courtship. He ran into an ambush from her family because he was much older than Martha Louisa

---

(4) Recalled by R. V. Neill, Springdale, Ark. Was about Bill von Berg's age at the time; the Neills were neighbors to the von Bergs and relatives of the Mayes' family.

(5) Walter Mayes, a nephew of Captain von Berg's wife, (who now lives on the old Mayes' place in the Mayfield Community in which was the von Berg ranch) tells this prank.

Mayes; and too he would soon be a divorced man as the legal proceedings had already been filed. But the Indian scout was used to ambushes, and having Martha Louisa on his side, (Martha's younger brother, John Mayes, was the pony express between Martha and Captain von Berg which resulted in a lasting friendship between the Captain and John) they won. So a month after his divorce was granted he and Martha were married April, 1889.[6]

Charlie Berg's wife was the favorite of the large Mayes family. She was Aunt Lou to all and this became her name to her many friends.

Bill continued to live with them and "come summer" the two pranksters were still at it. There was a stream below the house and it was hedged with thick growth. One part of this stream was particularly secluded and the right depth for the Captain to take his bath, which he did every day.

This was too good an opportunity for Bill to pass up. He slipped into a dress and sunbonnet of Aunt Lou's, while she was gathering eggs.

As Captain von Berg was enjoying his afternoon dip, the bushes parted and there stood a lady who in a shrill voice called to the Captain, "Is Aunt Lou up to the house?"

Bill said that the Captain came out of the creek so fast, he took most of the water with him. Then he had to laugh all over again before he could finish telling, "Looked like a waterspout. He then jumped into the bushes on the other side like a runaway horse."[7]

As a rancher, Charlie Berg wasn't. Bill and Aunt Lou looked after the ranch.

Captain von Berg's part-time occupation was a "whisky

---

(6) Marriage License, State of Arkansas, County of Washington, 29th day of April, 1889.

(7) J. W. Cannon, now living in Fayetteville, was a neighbor to the von Bergs when they lived at their ranch near Goshen and remembered the prank of Bill's.

gauger". There were some legitimate stills throughout that section of Arkansas and up into Missouri.

The old Captain would smack his lips as he said, "Westerners got to have their liquor." Then his blue eyes would twinkle as he added, "I find out who makes the best whisky."

His official status as a gauger is undetermined. His old neighbors and relatives of his wife's, state that he was a government gauger. The Internal Revenue Service said he may have been, or that he could have been an unofficial gauger for the distillers. The latter practice was abolished after 1896 by the Internal Revenue Laws.[8]

(Many years later when Joe Flanagan—Mrs. Ruth Mayes Flanagan's husband—went to work for a winery, he took the Captain's gauging stick with him, thinking that it might be of use to his company.)[9]

The von Berg ranch was about in the center of the distilleries he served in Arkansas (probably why he located there) and trips to them required at most a two-day period, however the ones in Missouri would take him away from home for about 10 days.

Upon returning from his jaunts Charlie Berg had a good listener, his wife. He would relate in "tall talk" fashion what he said and what they said, and no detail was too small to be excluded from his narratives.

Captain von Berg returning from one of his trips in Missouri launched into his highly descriptive, elongated relay of his journey. Bill was bored with this braggadocian talk. Bill stood as much as he could take and went out to do the chores, one of which was slopping the hogs. Sometime later

_____

(8) Letter dated August 6, 1965 from W. Neil Franklin, Chief Diplomatic, Legal, and Fiscal Branch, General Services Administration, Washington, D. C.

(9) The gauging stick was in the Mayes family (Flanagans, Springdale, Ark.) for many years.

when he returned the Captain was still going strong and Bill could not refrain from his urge: that of inverting the bucket in which he had carried out the slop to the hogs, over the Captain's head.

By the time the Captain extricated himself out from under the bucket, Bill was gone into the night and he stayed gone that night.[10]

One of his neighbors said of Captain von Berg, "He was a peculiar man. He was gentle and considerate of all wild life. Had pets of all kinds, even a deer. And his love for wild flowers was just as though they were little children.

"Then too, he was a peculiar man in that he didn't get along with his neighbors. Now Aunt Lou was the best neighbor anyone could have but Charlie Berg seemed like he was suspicious of his neighbors."[11]

This trait is quite understandable for in his years of outdoor life with the sky as his roof and nature as his neighbor he relaxed.

Too, he got along famously with the Indians but their habitat was what he was used to.

As Charles M. Russell, the famous painter of Indians, wrote:

"The Red man was the true American. They have almost all gone, but will never be forgotten. The history of how they fought for their country is written in blood, a stain that time cannot grind out. Their God was the sun; their church all out doors. Their only book was nature and they knew all the pages."[12]

Captain von Berg's pages were from his Lutheran prayer

---

(10) Bill von Berg evidently told Walter Mayes (who was a few years younger than Bill) about this. Bill probably spent that night with Walter.

(11) From tape recording by Ward Mayes, Meridian, Idaho. Ward was just a youngster at the time; was nephew of Aunt Lou.

(12) The Last Days of the Sioux Nation—Robert M. Utley.

book, which his mother had given him. He always carried this with him even when the trail and speed demanded "travel light."[13]

In 1891, Captain von Berg received a telegram from Buffalo Bill again urging him to join his show. He told Berg (as he called him) that the show was going to Europe and would play in Karlsruhe and other cities of Germany. He wired his regrets.

Ward Mayes, Aunt Lou's nephew (Ward was about 8 years old at the time) would spend the nights at the von Berg ranch when the Captain and Bill were away. "I liked to go over there," Ward said, "'cause they had lots of bees and that meant all the honey I could eat on Aunt Lou's fine dot biscuits."[14]

Bill and his father spent many happy days in the woods. The Indian scout pointed out tracks of wild life that Bill had stepped over unnoticed. He let Bill shoot first and then if he missed Captain von Berg shot his unerring way. This way he could correct Bill's aiming and shooting. The two called the trees by names so that Bill would know his timber with or without leaves. Wild flowers were rather reverently presented by senior von Berg. "Bill," he pointed out, "see those whippoorwill's shoes? (pitcher plant) Yah! They are blooming just for the two of us, for way off here in the hills, chances are no other mortal will set eyes on 'em."

It was on a bear hunt that Bill got furious at his father. They had made camp in just about a wilderness area. That day they had tramped until late afternoon and suddenly Bill found himself separated from his father.

He called and called but got no answer.

Bill said afterwards, "I was scart. I don't mind saying I was real scart 'cause my hair stood up."

---

(13) Miss Margaret A. Henry, Des Moines, Iowa, Captain von Berg's granddaughter, has his prayer book.

(14) Aunt Lou's dot biscuits probably were to Ward just dots compared with country biscuits cut out with a teacup.

Bill oriented his directions and tried to find their camp which he did. What he saw made him mad. There sat the Captain grinning at him.

But when his dad spoke it turned his anger into pride for his father said, "Bill, you'll do to tie to."

Jan. 15, 1898 the Department of the Interior, Bureau of Pensions, requested additional information of C. Louis von Berg which showed that he was receiving his Civil War Pension at that time.[15]

There was one painting which he made at the ranch which must have been somewhat like his pranks he played on his son, Bill. (It was signed C L v Berg 1898.) The painting was of one of his spotted ponies which showed good conformation. The saddle on the pony was a sidesaddle, almost photographically reproduced.

His wife (presumably) was holding the pony by the bridle reins. She was wearing her riding habit, a voluminous long skirt—not divided—which swept the ground, a shirtwaist, rather blousey and a sunbonnet. Her face was completely hidden by her sunbonnet.

In the foreground were two pincer dogs (as he called them—fox terriers).

When questioned about the painting as to why her face didn't show, Aunt Lou would laugh and that's all the explanation she gave.[16]

September 28, 1898, Buffalo Bill's Wild West Show performed at Fayetteville, Arkansas.

A clever line on Buffalo Bill's Wild West Show posters was, "Eleven hundred men and horses."

It was like a western rendezvous for Charlie Berg for

(15) Certificate No. 308896.

(16) Aunt Lou's niece, Mrs. Ruth Mayes Flanagan, Springdale, Ark. has this painting.

he visited with many of the performers—some were Indians—whom he had known in the West.

Colonel told Berg to bring his friends, that he had free reserved seats for them.

Over a hundred veterans in blue who had either been in the Western Army or the Civil War (Seventh Kansas Cavalry) with Colonel Cody formed a welcoming committee. The horses they rode were nondescript, not like the color matched mounts they had ridden in the U. S. Cavalry. Neither did their blue uniforms, although pressed for the occasion, have that ready for inspection look. Nontheless, their good spirit and welcome made up for what time had done to their figures and uniforms.

The portrayal of Custer's Last Battle at Little Big Horn was so realistic that it produced a grave hush among the over 10,000 attending the afternoon performance.

Miss Annie Oakley and Johnny Baker had star billing on the program.

Between the afternoon and night performances, Buffalo Bill went out with Charlie Berg to see his ranch and meet Aunt Lou. Said Ward Mayes, "I seed Buffalo Bill over at his house."[17]

The Fayetteville Democrat said of Buffalo Bill's Wild West Show in its next weekly edition, "Such exhibitions ought to be encouraged."[18]

John Mayes, Aunt Lou's younger brother was a frequent visitor at the ranch, "a-come-Saturday." He was teaching at Ribbon Ridge School House. His sister was mighty proud of her brother for he was studying law "of-a-nights." A lawyer friend in Fayetteville was lending him the law books. Captain von Berg commented, "John, that's the way Abe Lincoln did."

---

(17) Ward Mayes of Meridian, Idaho said this on a tape recording.
(18) Fayetteville Democrat issue of Sept. 29, 1898.

Nov. 24, 1903, Captain von Berg received a letter from W. F. Cody on The Irma Hotel stationery (Cody, Wyoming) —was named after his daughter—thanking him for a picture.[19]

Captain von Berg decided to move to Fayetteville (no doubt his "whisky gauging" had terminated). He made a number of trips there to pick out a site to build his lodge (as he called it). He selected a spot on a ledge about halfway up East Mountain, facing west. The town of Fayetteville below was in the valley and on knob hills.

In 1904, Captain von Berg and Aunt Lou moved into their new home. (Bill preferred to stay at the ranch.)

The first night in their new home, the town of Fayetteville either asleep or getting ready to retire, heard as the town clock was striking 9, TAPS—sounding clear and note perfect. It drifted like a fog down through the valleys and out toward the West. From that night on, at the hour of nine, Fayetteville and the surrounding area heard TAPS, regardless of the weather, as the Old Scout came out on his porch with his bugle.

When questioned as to why he blew TAPS, the Indian Scout spoke with feeling, "In honor of the many who fought and were killed to give us the West."

At his lodge Captain von Berg had a special room—in his plans it was to be his museum—and in it he placed all his mementoes, trophies, his paintings and other keepsakes from his West. Carlos Ludwig had some pieces he had brought to this country from Germany—German pipes, steins, his Lutheran prayer book and a painting of the von Berg's coat of arms. Louis von Berg was represented too with some relics from the War Between the States.

There was a sign over the outside door, "von Berg Museum, admission 25 cents". If the Old Scout ever charged anyone who came halfway up the mountain to see his museum and to see him, I never knew of it. For with gesture

---

(19) Letter in von Berg Collection, University of Arkansas Museum.

of his hands he would refuse to take the money. "Yah! It's just a joke," he would say, "that sign." [20]

The von Bergs had just moved into their new home.

Aunt Lou was "stewing," it being Saturday and her brother, John, had not been up to visit them.

She kept going to the window, watching for him. About dusk she recognized her brother starting up the mountain.

John arrived out of breath and terribly excited.

His sister and the Captain were quite solicitous.

"Wait 'till I get my hat off," he joshed, "and I'll tell you. I came in early this morning to return some law books and get others. My lawyer teacher jumped me about taking the bar examination. Said that the bar was meeting this morning.

"I told him I didn't feel that I was quite ready to take the examination.

" 'Well, come on,' he urged, 'we'll go up on the square to the Court House and it will give you some experience as to what you can expect on examinations.'

"I asked him if taking this examination and failing it might count against me when I came up the second time.

" 'No, it won't,' he assured me.

"Was I scared. There were judges and lawyers facing me, six of 'em, all distinguished men. I felt like I imagine how our old sow felt when she got caught under the garden gate.

"One of the members of the bar popped the first question to me.

"I studied a short while and then gave my answer.

" 'Wrong,' exclaimed one of the lawyers.

" 'He's absolutely right,' proclaimed one of the judges.

(20) Sunday Magazine—St. Louis Post-Dispatch—October 7, 1917 verified this.

"The other four spoke out, in turn, two of them said I was wrong and two said I was right.

"Well, they argued and argued between themselves until they got hungry and we quit for dinnah.

"After dinnah they went at it again and their arguments continued until late afternoon. All I did was just sit there and listen.

"Finally one of the members of the bar said, 'Gentlemen, it's getting late; I have to get home and milk my cow.'

"So they agreed to stop.

"Then one of the attorneys asked, 'What about this young man?'

"I felt I already knew about this young man. I would be reprimanded and told not to come back until I had learned my lessons.

"Another spoke up, 'Anyone,' and he repeated, 'anyone, who can propound an answer that has taken us all day to try and decide whether he was right should be admitted to our bar.'

"The other five fell right in with him. The next thing I knew they were shaking my hand as a new member of the Washington County Bar.[21]

---

(21) a. Lawyer John Mayes told this to the writer years ago.

b. Chancery Record, Washington County, Vol. G Page 173: John Mayes, Ex Parte: Comes in this day John Mayes, and presents to the Court his application, supported by affidavit of L. W. Gregg as to moral character of petitioner, for a license to practice law in the State of Arkansas in the Circuit, Chancery and inferior Courts in said State, and said applicant being examined in manner and form as prescribed by law and being found to possess the necessary qualifications of learning and ability to entitle him to a license to practice law in the Circuit, Chancery and inferior Courts of the State of Arkansas as counsellor at Law, and Solicitor in Chancery.

It is by the Court, ordered, adjudged and decreed that the said John Mayes be and he is licensed to practice Law in the Circuit, Chancery and inferior Court of the State of Arkansas, and the said John Mayes in open Court took the oath required by Law.

"Lawyer Mayes is moving to Fayetteville, Martha," he joyously added.

From his front porch where on a clear day Captain von Berg could see into the Indian Territory—always to him—he enjoyed painting. His inspirations came from the ever-changing panorama. Too, his photographic mind recalled incidents and places in the West which he put on canvases.

The Old Scout was about his paintings as he was about the admission charge to his museum.

"Come Decoration Day," Captain von Berg was there on horseback, marshal of the parade.

His old horse was not recognized by the crowd for he was prancing, cakewalking, his head up now that he was back with the militia.

The marshal too was old but the way he sat in the saddle, his soldier bearing and his blue army uniform, neatly pressed, gave him that active service look. Only his visage was that of a veteran.

As he stoically led off the parade, whether he was living again the rear guard charge in the Red River campaign; or making ready to reach for a "chaw" of tobacco before the Indians approached close enough to shoot; or snaking out under fire to bring back a wounded scout, only Captain von Berg knew.

The Old Scout, after the ceremonies in the National Cemetery, joshing with a veteran said, "Yah! Guess I better pick me out a spot."

Captain von Berg received a letter dated Oct. 12, 1906 from Captain Jack Crawford, "The Poet Scout."[22]

In it he referred to a previous visit with Captain von Berg. Captain Jack Crawford who had been with Colonel

---

(22) Letter in von Berg Collection, University of Arkansas Museum.

Cody in various show enterprises was now a celebrity in his own status. On his letterhead he showed a bust of himself quite monumental with western lore.

Now he was on a circuit and his letter stated: "Have most of my time sold for next summer and am sold for this winter." He followed this with, "I hope some day to meet you again. Give my regard to any of the Old Timers who like yourself have seen actual service." Then he let himself go, "The Posers of Dime Novel Buffalo Bill monstrositys are painful to behold but white people love to be humbugged. They will put their good money to see a Barnum fake rather than to see a real class of men who never brag about Indians they killed."

In Captain von Berg's museum was an Indian war bonnet of a Blackfoot and the scalp that went with it. This Indian had given von Berg a souvenir which the Captain carried with him day and night for years. It was a tip of an arrowhead embedded in his leg. At his lodge—Fayetteville didn't have a hospital at that time—using the dining room table as an operating table, Dr. E. F. Ellis—a famous Arkansas physician—removed this tip of the arrowhead. Captain von Berg administered his own anesthetic which was whisky —one stiff drink before the operation and more to come as the pain intensified.[23]

Major Wm. A. Bell and his young son, Cody Bell, visited Captain von Berg and his wife in the early part of 1907.

This was when the picture was taken of the three, Wm. A. Bell, Cody Bell and Captain von Berg, with the caption, "When shall we three meet again?"

Cody Bell, who was for his age a good musician was intrigued with the Captain blowing taps at 9 o'clock. To Cody, the highlight of his visit was the Captain taking time to instruct him on blowing the bugle.

When Major Bell returned home to Sigourney, Iowa he

---

(23) Arkansas Gazette, Nov. 1, 1964.

wrote and published his *Echoes from the Mountains to the Plains,* May 1, 1907. In his foreword Major Bell had this to say:

"Having been so interested in my visit, and to return the compliments of the good time shown me by my old friend, I can only extend my friendship to the Captain and his lovely wife with this little souvenir, as a token of my friendship and remembrance of times that can never return to us again. I should be pleased to give a longer history of my old friend if time would only permit me. As it is, I have to give a short review, such as I remembered as we were relating our life in the West. Should I be able to write a true history of the Captain's life it would make a large volume. I have illustrated the Souvenir such as I think would please Captain von Berg and his friends."

In one of Major Bell's illustrations in his *Echoes from the Mountains to the Plains* is a picture with the following caption:

"A Christmas Day Scene in the home of Col. Wm. F. Cody on his TE Ranch in the Pahaska Mountains, on the banks of the Shoshone river. The party consists of Col. Cody, his sister, Mrs. Goodman, Frank S. Yeager and the writer. Cody Bell and Walter Goodman in a quiet Western game. Photo taken in 1905."

A large painting on the wall in the above picture appears to be one of Captain von Berg's, showing a bivouac of scouts in the woods.

Charlie Berg made a trip back to Iowa and wanted Aunt Lou to go with him but under the circumstances she didn't go as, of course, Le Mars would be on his itinerary.[24]

1910, Captain von Berg and Aunt Lou adopted a baby boy. He was named Jack Crawford.

(Bill von Berg had long since gone back to Iowa.)

---

(24) Le Mars Weekly Sentinel, March 12, 1918: "Mr. Berg paid a visit to Le Mars a few years ago and met many old cronies."

Jack Crawford von Berg wrote many years later very tenderly of his foster parents:

"The old captain and his good wife tended and nourished the tiny infant through its years. On his wife's lap I learned the true story of Jesus Christ, Our Savior. From my earliest remembrances I would listen to the Old Warrior recount his past days of battle and glory. Hand in hand he walked with me into the dense woods at that time abounding East Mountain. He showed me the ways of nature, manliness and to walk straight and tall with head proudly high.

"And they named him Jack Crawford von Berg, the Jack Crawford being the name of a hunting crony of the Captain's."[25]

Everytime Able James McAllister came down from Iowa to visit his son, Dr. B. F. McAllister, he and his grandson, Max would walk up East Mountain for a visit with Captain von Berg. When he arrived at the von Berg home, he was Private McAllister and the Old Scout was Private von Berg, for they had soldiered together in the Iowa contingent.[26]

The following letter dated, "Sept. 27, Evening (no year given) Lexington, Ky." was received by Captain von Berg. It was written on *Buffalo Bill's Wild West* stationery.

"Dear Old Friend

You will be very much astonished to know that I am writing you, in Col. Cody private tent on his private writing table, and the Col. is sitting at my right smoking between his part in the big show watching the Indians and Cowboys make their entrance to the show. Have had a fine visit with

---

(25) Excerpts from letters written by Jack Crawford von Berg, West Milford, West Virginia to the writer.

(26) a. His grandson, Max, is Dr. Max F. McAllister and lives in Fayetteville.

b. Roster and Record of Iowa Soldiers in the War of the Rebellion 1861-1866. Courtesy of Carnegie-Stout Free Public Library, Dubuque, Iowa.

the Col. and he is the old Boy as of old, the Col. said to give his best regards and when he gets home to the mountains he is going to look up the painting you sent him 3 years or so ago, he said, he did not get it not saying it was not delivered but so many things are and has been sent that he don't always get to see them for persons receiving them for him overlook reporting everything. He said he was going to look up the painting. He now thanks you very much for the same through my correspondence. I am just getting ready for a ride in the old stage coach.

With best regard, from myself & the Col.

Wm. A. Bell"[27]

A telegram Jan. 10, 1917 brought Captain von Berg the sad news that Colonel W. F. Cody, Buffalo Bill, had died.

He wired his condolence and regrets that he could not come as he was in failing health.

His good friend, Wm. A. Bell, later sent him excellent photographs of the last rite atop Lookout Mountain near Denver, which he had taken.

Anyone who has climbed Lookout Mountain can appreciate the magnitude of the crowd that was there for the graveside service.

Although Buffalo Bill's body had lain in state in the rotunda of the State Capitol in Denver, there were many atop Lookout Mountain that day who had not seen that last rite. So contrary to the arrangements the casket was opened (family's request).[28]

Major Wm. A. Bell was there with the Cody family as Captain von Berg would have been if he had been well

(27) Letter in the von Berg Collection, University of Arkansas Museum.

(28) Photograph showing the open casket and the long line passing before the bier. This photograph along with the others are in possession of Mrs. Ruth Mayes Flanagan, Springdale, Ark.

enough to have made the trip. Mike Russell was there too. (It was from his ranch that the TE brand originated.)[29]

The Old Scout pointed out Cody Boal in one of the pictures. "He was the Colonel's favorite grandson," he informed Aunt Lou.

Captain von Berg never rallied back to his very self after Buffalo Bill's death.

The TAPS at nine no longer floated over the town, valleys and through the gap to the West beyond.

It was a warm day in the Indian summer. The panorama was painted in colors like no artist could put on canvas. The trees waved their colored leaves—some "maple red," yellow gold and the combination of these with leftover summer green as though hand painted (the maples), some leathery red and brown (the oaks) and others still green. In this setting Aunt Lou supported the ailing Old Scout out on the porch down the steps to a chair placed in the yard. She said, she would be right back. While she was gone the Old Scout scanned the panorama as though taking a good stiff drink of his whisky.

Presently Aunt Lou returned and on her head was an Indian war bonnet, the feathers trailing behind like a train. She then danced in a circle around the "Old Warrior" (as Jack Crawford von Berg fondly referred to his foster father).

The Old Scout laughed and chuckled between weak war whoops which he could give as well as a Sioux could.[30]

March 2, 1918, the Old Scout died.[31]

Some said that night at 9 o'clock they distinctly heard TAPS.

---

(29) Mike Russell was identified on the back of one of the pictures in Major Wm. A. Bell's handwriting.

(30) Tape recording of Ward Mayes, Meridian, Idaho. He was a nephew of Aunt Lou's.

(31) Certificate of Death, General Services Administration, National Archives and Records Service, Washington, D. C.

The Fayetteville Democrat (which was a daily then) reported, "The Boy Scouts proteges of the Old Scout attended the service in a body and marched in the procession (Author: dirt road—no paved streets in the town then—and over a mile) from the church to the National Cemetery."[32]

"Scouts don't say goodbye,
but bis dann."[33]

(32) Front page, Fayetteville Democrat, March 4, 1918.

(33) "Be seeing you."

INDEX